RIDING
LESSONS

RIDING LESSONS

Everything That Matters in Life I Learned from Horses

BO DEREK

WITH MARK SEAL

ReganBooks
An Imprint of HarperCollins*Publishers*

HarperCollins books may be purchased for educational, business, or sales promotional use. For information please write: Special Markets Department, HarperCollins Publishers Inc., 10 East 53rd Street, New York, NY 10022.

FIRST EDITION

Designed by Kris Tobiassen

Printed on acid-free paper

Library of Congress Cataloging-in-Publication Data has been applied for.

ISBN 0-06-039437-4

02   03   04   05   06   ❖/RRD   10   9   8   7   6   5   4   3   2   1

For Bobby

RIDING
LESSONS

ONE

"Fuck, Chuck, not another infomercial!"

Chuck is my manager, and he's forever phoning with "business opportunities" that always seem to be in regard to one "opportunity" I've always avoided: infomercials. All I have to do to get rich quick is to spend one lousy day pitching the public to buy one more thing that nobody needs. Everything from the latest vitamins, to the "Perfect 10" vacation sweepstakes, to an honest-to-God miracle antiaging cream, to the best ab-flattener you will never use, to a sexual enhancement drug—excuse me, "dietary supplement." You see, the U.S. government regulates drugs and won't let you make dishonest claims about them.

Today, Chuck's phone call finds me sitting on my mare, Gaiata, in Ramon Becerras's riding arena about ten minutes from my home near Santa Barbara. It's a wonderful, funky place. One side resembles a Western streetfront, the other has a saloon where we often ride right up to the bar for mounted shots of tequila. There's also a pool table so we can play billiards on horseback like Billy the Kid did.

3

I listen to Chuck's pitch for the infomercial a while longer, and lie to him that I'll think about it, then push End on my cell phone and clip it back to my jeans.

The Spanish music is cranked up loud. For the past hour, I've been trying to persuade Gaiata that we would both look very cute if we would do a pretty pirouette when we reach the center of the arena. She's not buying it. I must be doing something wrong. It's my fault. It's *always* my fault. It takes all of my concentration to ride her well, and now this phone call from Chuck isn't helping at all. I feel a tequila break coming on.

The phone rings again. "Yes, Chuck," I say, knowing it's him.

"I forgot to tell you one thing," he says. "The offer is good only for two more hours. Then they'll offer it to someone else."

What is it with these infomercial people? Why do they keep coming to me? When will they get the message: *I don't want to do it.*

I know in my heart I'm going to turn it down even as I pretend that I am considering it. Poor Chuck, I'm wasting his time. And why do I have such a low opinion of infomercials and Home Shopping Network and QVC and Value Vision anyway? As though I will lose a piece of my soul if I do just one.

Last week Chuck called and said, "There's this guy, he's kind of a creep, but he wants to give you $250,000 just to use your picture on the Web to sell his hotel."

It's not that I don't need the money. Just the opposite. I'm close to broke. Actually, worse than that: I'm about to go into debt again. I just sent in my tax return, but I can't pay my taxes. Well, I could if I cashed out, but there is an impending actor's strike, and I think I'd better hold on to the last of my money. I swore to myself that I would never, ever go into debt again, that debt was part of my past life. And now, I can't believe it: I'm about to owe the Internal Revenue Service one more time!

I did some really shitty films recently in order to earn a respectable amount of money, like *Horror 101* ("With Bo Derek as Miss James, the teacher who murders her whole class by locking her students in the freezer!"). But almost as quick as the credits rolled, the money was all gone. I don't spend much. I rent a modest house with my sister and her family. My car is four years old. Expensive clothes mean nothing to me. Neither does jewelry. So where did it all go?

Chuck calls back. "I don't understand, you said that you need the money."

"I do, but . . ."

"Look, if it hits, it's a million dollars a year for you."

I look down at my motionless mare and think, *It's a good thing I'm not trying to sell an exercise machine to Gaiata today. I wouldn't make a penny.*

"Chuck, can't you get me a real job?"

"Yeah, any day now something's going to break," he says. "You've been getting good press lately. People are talking about you."

"That's just because I'm a widow," I say. "They would look really bad if they were mean to me now." Again I promise Chuck that I'll think about the infomercial.

The common perception about being a widow is true. Ever since my husband, John, died in 1998, I can tell you that our society is really nice to widows. Even *People* magazine is nice to me now, and they beat me up for twenty years.

Basically, I'm the same person I've always been. Except, of course, that I am no longer controlled by my self-promoting Svengali, Pygmalion, pimp of a husband. That's what the press called him. But they never got it: If John had been a self-promoting Svengali, Pygmalion, pimp of a husband, he would have left me a fortune!

What is wrong with me? I'm way too old to be turning down this kind of money. It's one thing when you are young and have your whole career ahead of you. But now? These are the times when I feel most alone. No one is going to provide for me, and no one is going to make decisions for me.

I suppose some would think my hesitation to leap wallet-first into the valley of infomercials has something to do with my husband's beyond-the-grave influence on me. He certainly took the blame the twenty-five years we were together.

"John, you're an idealist," friends would say. "You don't live in the real world! You don't care about money, but Bo is young! You won't always be around to take care of her. Please, John, let her go and make some money!"

To be honest, I always wondered about this myself. But since he's been gone, I haven't once thought to myself, *What would John say? What would John want me to do?* My decisions are my own, just as they have always been.

I have this strong aversion to selling something I don't believe in. It's my nature. I wish I could get off my high horse, get rid of these old-fashioned, outdated principles that have no place in today's grab-it-while-you-can world.

It won't happen today. No, today I will go back to what I care about more than anything else: connecting in some meaningful way with the beautiful creature between my legs: Gaiata. Today I will ask so much of her, ask her to leave her equine world and join mine. And if I am very good today—if I am a true horsewoman—she will be happy that I pulled her away from her green grass, her friends, and everything that makes her life happy and secure.

As for my own situation, I know this new financial crisis will resolve itself and that I won't have much to do with the outcome. I have been far too lucky in life to believe that I have ever been in control. My opportunities are still undeserved, gifts from somewhere, maybe the gods. In the Mel Brooks comedy *History of the World: Part I,* the ill-fated King Louis XVI of France says "It's good to be king." True, but I would argue that it's better to be Bo. Life has played some funny tricks on me and taken me on a wild ride. How did I ever get into this wonderful mess that is my life?

"Come on, Gaiata," I say. "Pretty please with sugar on it? One little pirouette?"

My attempt is an ugly, sloppy turn; far from fitting within a "space the size of a plate," which King Friedrich II of Prussia considered the correct form for a pirouette.

"Ramon!" I say. "She feels hard."

Ramon, a master trainer and Hollywood stunt rider, calls out to me, "You're tense. You're making her hard! Back her up, across the whole arena. Get her mouth off the bit and trot. Go back to the basics for a while. Back to the beginning."

I hate to trot, but around and around the arena I must go. Back to the basics, the beginning. Ramon is right. The only way to get Gaiata collected and centered again so that she can function properly is to trot her until she is going in a relaxed, natural gait.

I feel the same way about me. I'm running. Not thinking, just working and going and doing. I'm off balance. Not centered. Not supple and soft. Not poised to go in any direction. I've got the bit in my teeth, and I'm just running. Maybe I should take Ramon's advice for myself and get back to the basics. Back to the beginning . . .

I was born Mary Cathleen Collins, the oldest of three girls and a boy. And I was born horse crazy. I believe that someday, after scientists have broken the genetic code to cure disease, they will begin to discover what makes us individuals. Why some of us have special callings. Why certain children are drawn to musical instruments. I know that I possess the gene that makes me one of the millions of females who were born with an inexplicable passion for horses.

There is no logical explanation for my obsession. My parents were not farm people; I grew up near the beach in the concrete suburbs of southern California. My mother recalls that I would spend hours on my rocking horse; that plastic horse was like a drug to me.

As a girl I had a recurring dream. I don't know when it started. It seems I've always had it. I'm standing on top of a hill, an outcropping that overlooks a beautiful valley. The sun must be going down, because the sky is blazing pink. I'm standing next to a beautiful stallion. He is a palomino, my absolute favorite type of horse when I was a girl. After all, Roy Rogers's Trigger was a palomino; so was Thunderhead, son of Flicka.

Palominos are blonds. Some are brassy, some are strawberry, but the stallion in my dream has a dark, rich coat dappled with a sooty cast. His mane and tail are pale, almost white, like my own long hair. We are standing side by side looking out over the valley. He sees something and lets out a cry; an imperious, penetrating, and very deep, chesty neigh. Then he exhales explosively through his nose. This is his alarm. A stallion's blow will chill you to the bone.

He tosses his head toward me and rolls his eyes back. He is telling me that we have to go down to the valley. I grab a good hunk of his mane, swing up onto his bare back, and we're off at a gallop. I ride him effortlessly. We are going so fast that his mane blows back and tickles my face and gets tangled in my own hair until you can't tell which is which. He loves me, and I know it. He would prefer to be with me than with another horse, and I would rather be with him than with anyone else, including my family. If I don't wake up, I know that we could live together in this beautiful valley forever, just my stallion and me.

Funny, there was never a Prince Charming in my dream. I know that most little girls dream of Prince Charming, but not me. And when I read fairy tales, I was always more interested in the horse Prince Charming was riding in the illustrations.

When I went outside to play on the sidewalk, I played Horse. I galloped and cantered, and I knew exactly how many paces there were between each of the neighborhood fences I jumped. I would carry a stick—my imaginary riding crop—and I would give my own thigh a sharp slap as I approached the jump. I whinnied and neighed and nickered.

Eventually the bedroom that I shared with my two younger sisters became covered with horse "porn": glossy centerfolds of horses in all sorts of appealing positions. Only the ones with the best legs and chests would go up on my wall.

I have a faded photograph of me at about four years old on my first pony. A man used to earn his living by going door to door with a pony, a camera, and a trunk full of costumes, hoping to find mothers with horse-crazy little girls like me. I can see in the photo that I have chosen the cowgirl costume. I'm sure that the man had an English riding outfit as well, for the girls who wanted to be like Velvet Brown (the character played by a young Elizabeth Taylor in the movie *National Velvet*), but I was always a cowgirl. I have on boots with pointed toes, chaps with beautiful silver conchos down the sides, a fringed leather vest, and, of course, a cowgirl hat with the stampede strings done up tight under my chin. My left hand is held up as if to say "Howdy, pardner!"

Most of all, I notice the smile: that just-about-to-burst grin of pure joy. I still catch myself with that very same grin today, and I have to say it looks kind of goofy on a forty-four-year-old woman. But there is nothing I can do about it. It doesn't happen as often as it used to. But I occasionally feel pure joy.

A woman is like a tea bag. You never know how
strong she is until you get her into hot water.

—ELEANOR ROOSEVELT

My mother gave me this quote in a little silver picture frame on the day my husband died. I keep it by my bathroom sink and look at it every day as I brush my teeth. And on those days when I feel as though I will drown in the hot water, this simple, beautiful thought reminds me that I survived a very bad day. It reminds me that I'm tough!

On May 25, 1998, I ordered the life support to be turned off after my husband suffered aortic dissection. Or as the doctor put it, catastrophic heart failure. No matter how you prepare for such a moment, no matter the living wills you sign, it's still surreal and ugly and macabre when it actually happens. John and I used to joke about it. If I talked about something too far in the future, he'd say, "Shit! You'll be pushing my wheelchair by then." Planting seedling trees was a sore subject with him. He was thirty years older than me; barring an accident, he would die before me. I didn't like to think about it much, because, of course, I would be so "old" by then—in my *forties!*

My girlfriend Layla drove me home from the hospital where John died. Home was our forty-five-acre horse ranch in a beautiful valley north of Santa Barbara, California. We had an enormous, seven-thousand-square-foot house, over one hundred oak trees, some twenty-six horses, one donkey, nine dogs, three cats, and a parrot.

As we drove through the gates, I remember thinking, *It—John's death, his passing—has really happened.* I don't know why I keep referring to his death as *it*. I suppose because it was bound to happen. We had been together for twenty-five years. This was the moment that I had signed on for. *It* didn't feel especially dramatic or life changing; it still doesn't most of the time. Just something that happened.

What a gorgeous day it was! We sat outside near my vegetable garden and stared out at the view.

"Bo, I'm going to miss John so much," said Layla. "I feel like I've lost a girlfriend."

I looked at her, puzzled.

"Not that John was unmasculine," she continued. "But I could share things with him that I would never speak about to another husband of one of my girlfriends. He was just . . . *interested*."

"I understand what you mean," I said. "John loved you. He loved women."

I could see some of my horses grazing on the hills. *How strange*, I thought. I felt fine. I wasn't crying or screaming, as I'd imagined I would. Actually, I felt quite numb.

Then the storm hit. So many people began to arrive, coming to give me support, to be there for me. I was overwhelmed at how people cared about me and worried about how I was feeling and handling *it*. I had never realized how much John meant to so many people.

There was much food and frivolity. I was amazed at how our friends could eat and laugh. You'd think we were all having a wild party. I suppose they ate and laughed so much out of nervousness. But occasionally I would stop and look around and think, *Is everyone supposed to be having so much fun?*

It was getting late in the day, and I remember feeling the dread of night coming on. *Eventually*, I thought, *all these people are going to go home. It's going to be very quiet, and I am going to be alone. I'll have to go upstairs to bed. Oh no, too spooky! I might start thinking about things, about* it. *Thank God for sleeping pills. At least I won't have to think tonight.*

Kerry, my baby sister, interrupted my thoughts. "You have your whole life to grieve," she kept telling me. "You don't have to do it right now."

"But then what?" I asked. "What about everything?"

"What do you mean?" she asked. "The ranch?"

"Yes."

"Don't worry," she said. "We're moving in tonight."

And that was that. Kerry talked to her husband, and they and their two children moved in that very night. I was blessed with not having to live alone or come home to an empty house.

Before bed, I went down to the barn to see my horse Mouro. My barn was not one of those prefabricated port-a-barns so popular and affordable now. This was the real thing, built of wood and plaster, with a graceful, sloping Spanish tile roof. My six stallions lived there; I'd midwifed two of them when they were born, or *foaled*. The barn was also home to rattlesnakes, mice, and, thanks to a healthy colony of eave-dwelling Mexican brown bats, not too many bugs. But there were plenty of tarantulas and so many other things that used to scare me when I first moved to the country. I soon came to accept them, to appreciate that they were all part of what made this part of the ranch my favorite place. The place with the wonderful smells: a combination of leather, alfalfa, molasses, manure, and a touch of ammonia from the urine. And the dirt—it permeated everything. I could measure how good my day at the barn was by how much dirt I washed off in the shower at night.

As I entered Mouro's stall, he looked over at me briefly, dismissively, then returned his gaze out the window. He was a handsome Lusitano stallion of a very old, rare bloodline from Portugal. A silvery gray, he wasn't fancy to the untrained eye; he didn't have a lot of mane and tail. No, Mouro was all bone structure, pride, and gusto. He was the most dominant of my stallions. In the eighteen years we were together, I have to admit he was my favorite.

"My day was really shitty, Mouro," I said. "How was yours?"

He gave me a quick glance with his big brown eye that looked like melted chocolate.

"Did that other horse get too close to you today?" I asked. "Did you have to go to every corner of your pasture and shit to mark your territory? Oh, I bet you were so fierce . . ."

He wasn't listening to me at all. He never had much time to be affectionate or cuddly. But I knew I'd touched him somewhere in his horse soul. Whenever I'd leave him, he would scream and kick the wall of his stall. He was such a stud horse, a man's man, always keeping an eye on the horizon for danger or threats—or maybe if he was lucky, a mare.

"Oh, Mouro! What do I do now?" I asked.

He stood still for the longest time while I cried into his neck.

TWO

There is something about riding down the street
on a prancing horse that makes you feel
like something, even when you ain't a thing.

—WILL ROGERS

My first real adventure on a horse happened when I was about
eleven. We were living in a tract house in Torrance, California, a
suburb sandwiched between the intersection of three major L.A.
freeways. It's an interesting area where all of Los Angeles once
dumped its garbage until the area was reclaimed and covered over
with factories and baby boomer dream houses.

Who knows what seeped up through the ground? This was long
before the environmental regulations we have today. Everyone in my
family jokes that we glow in the dark. The air usually smelled like
cooked cabbage from the nearby Harvey's Aluminum plant, or like
coffee (which smelled wonderful) from the nearby Farmers Coffee
factory. Home ownership was every family's dream, and my father
had used his GI Bill to buy our fifteen-hundred-square-foot home in
1962 for nineteen thousand dollars. We were all very proud of it.

Our ears were always extrasharp in the middle of the afternoon,
listening for the ice-cream man. One day I heard hoofbeats outside

on the street. As impossible as it seemed, a horse was out there walking, or somebody had two coconut shells they were banging together. I ran through the house, screaming hysterically, "A horse! A horse!" My siblings and I collided at the door at the same time. I pushed my brother, Colin, away and screamed, "Let me go first! I'm the one who loves horses!" I was the oldest, and a shameless bully.

I ran out, looked up the street, and there he was: Archibald, the most beautiful horse I had ever seen. He was a palomino, of course. He was a real horse, too, not a little pony. The horse belonged to Jan, a girl who lived up the street. She was offering rides on Archibald to help her pay for his feed and board. I still remember the prices: a nickel for a walk and a dime for a trot. Either way, all customers rode bareback because Jan couldn't afford a saddle.

I had never gotten to know Jan well. She was quiet and older than I was—in *high school!*—so she didn't bother with me. I soon fixed that. I became her very best friend, kissed her bottom relentlessly, and finally convinced her that she could trust me with Archibald. I told her that I was a great rider (totally untrue), knew all about horses (also untrue), and could give rides for her on the weekends.

Archibald lived in a dry, barren little pen about three miles away. Every Saturday and Sunday we used to coax Archie from his pen with carrots and apples. Then we walked him back along four-lane Torrance Boulevard to our street, because Mom let us ride him only on the smaller streets around our house, where kids would line up for rides. What a different time it was! Can you imagine letting your child give an eleven-year-old girl a dime to go trotting off down the asphalt on the back of a horse, with no saddle or helmet? Those were the days before lawyers and lawsuits prevented kids from having fun (and breaking their necks).

I got pretty cocky being the Chosen One to handle Archie. Whenever he wasn't in service earning his keep, I was on his back—riding, resting, but mostly showing off. I loved to trot down the street where little kids would come running out to see us. Occasionally I had to give my brother a ride; that was in exchange for him following us with a shovel to pick up Archie's manure. None of us had ever had a lesson in riding or horse husbandry. We learned the old-fashioned way: by doing.

Always in search of the magnificent stallion from my dream, I began imagining that Archie really loved me more than Jan. He told me so every time he tossed his head and rolled his eyes in my direction. Our rides down the street got more and more daring.

Late one afternoon, *way* too close to feeding time, I gave him a little kick. Well, old Archie took off back to the barn like a bolt of lightning. A runaway horse on pavement is a very serious thing. His steel shoes are slippery and it's a dangerous situation for the horse and the screaming brat with her nails dug into his back. The more I screamed, the faster those coconut shells kept clopping. I pulled back on the reins as hard as I could, but Archie just stuck out his jug head and ran even faster. I had no control at all. My brother and sisters were left far behind, running after me and flailing their arms, screaming at me to come back.

We were coming up fast on Normandie Avenue, four lanes at rush hour. But before the intersection stood an elevated train track built up on an earthen berm. I figured that would stop Archie. He was breathing hard now and had broken a sweat. His back was wet and slick, which made it really hard to hold on. I let go of the reins, grabbed his neck, and held on for my life. He charged on and took the berm like a steeplechase horse! As we reached the top, I could feel in my seat that he intended to take the boulevard—and its traffic—next.

As Archie leapt off the tracks and into the air, I decided, enough was enough: I was going to die. It was time to bail. I passed out. Fainting has become something of a comfort to me. Throughout my life, whenever things get too scary, I faint. When I awoke, I was staring up at the front bumper of a car. I could smell the burning rubber from half a dozen cars that had come screeching to a halt. I could see Archie all lathered up, prancing around, his tail preened up over his back, spooking and shying at the cars and the people who were trying to catch him. He took off down the boulevard, back in the direction of his pen (and dinner) bucking and farting and feeling very pleased with himself.

People were very upset. I heard someone say he would call the police and an ambulance. The driver of the car that nearly hit me was pale and nervous as he helped me up. My brother and sisters came running up wailing that they thought I was going to die. As for me, I felt a little stiff. I found a few cuts and bruises. I was limping, but nothing was seriously wrong. I've always had a very high pain threshold. My first thought was to get out of there fast. If the police came, they would tell my mom, and she would never let me ride Archie again.

I assured everyone that I was fine and told my brother and sisters to knock off the crying. We started running down the boulevard in search of Archie. We found him at the gate to his pen, hot and dripping with sweat, waiting for dinner as though nothing had happened. We had to cool him off and groom him to hide the evidence of what happened, because if Jan saw Archie dusted white with salt from his dried sweat, she would know that I had run him too hard, and she too would never let me ride Archie again.

Never again would I hang on to a runaway horse. Whenever it became obvious that I would lose control—*Dingdong!*—a little bell went off in my head. *If I had jumped off Archibald, I wouldn't have ended up under the bumper of that car.*

"Jump before you get thrown." It's a lesson I could apply to my life.

Ann-Margret will be absolutely furious with me for telling this story. She's so secretive and modest and has never, ever mentioned her place in my life. But she was there.

My father with
Ann-Margret and
one of her first
putt-putts, during
Kitten with a Whip.

My father first met Ann-Margret while teaching her to ride a motorcycle in 1963, when he supplied all the bikes for her movie *Bye Bye Birdie*. Ann-Margret had loved motorcycles since she was a little girl in Sweden, where her favorite uncle, Calle, used to give her rides on the back of his. During the course of filming *Bye Bye Birdie*, her then boyfriend, Eddie Fisher, bought a Honda minibike from my father and presented it to Ann-Margret as a birthday gift. She was a great rider and very soon outgrew her little putt-putt, so Dad upgraded her to a Honda 150, which didn't satisfy her for long either.

A-M's friendship with my mother and father grew as she worked her way up the cc (engine size, in cubic centimeters) ladder. Eventually she was riding a Triumph 500. It was a huge, powerful bike for her five-foot-four frame, and she just wasn't big enough or strong enough to kick-start it. So my father had the bike modified with an electric starter, making it the only one of its kind in existence for years. A-M's passion for big bikes hasn't faded a bit. Last time I looked, she still had three really hot Harleys in her just-for-the-motorcycles garage.

I was introduced to her when I was nine years old, and I fell completely under her spell when she said in her soft, husky, Ann-Margret voice, "Hi, Cathy!" Although both my parents are very good-looking, Ann-Margret was everything gorgeous and glamorous to me. She was voluptuous, whereas my mom was slim—a body type not in fashion then as it is now (lucky for me, since I am built like my mom). She wore beautiful, stylish clothes in pretty, bright colors. Her makeup and hair were always perfect.

From the day I met her, I idolized A-M. When my friends didn't want to play horse anymore, I would compromise and play *movie star* with them, but only if I could be Ann-Margret. I would fight with any other little girl who wanted to be her. She was mine.

By the time actor Roger Smith and A-M married, the Collins family was spending most weekends up at the Smith house in Benedict Canyon just above Beverly Hills, which was considered wilderness in those days. The house was a lovely, happy, classic white wooden California ranch–style home on seven acres. It once belonged to Humphrey Bogart and Lauren Bacall. I actually have a picture of my John walking out its front door arm-in-arm with Bogey and Betty in 1949. The house was built up on a hill, which meant that it had a long asphalt driveway—*perfect* for riding motorcycles.

Roger had three children from a previous marriage: Tracy, a girl my age; Jordan, a boy my brother's age; and little Dallas, the youngest boy, who fell between my sisters' ages. It was all so convenient. My parents and Roger and A-M could enjoy one another's company while we kids entertained ourselves. Being the oldest, Tracy and I were "in charge." We were supposed to watch over the others. Ha! Most of the time we just got the little ones in trouble.

We all had motorcycles, starting with a couple of 75ccs, down to cute little minibikes for the five-year-olds. We even had a minibike with a sidecar that my father had built for chimpanzees to drive on a television show. The chimps were better at driving it than I was. I kept forgetting that the sidecar was there, misjudging my extra width and sideswiping the fence or a tree until finally no one would ride with me.

The Smiths' long driveway was our racecourse. Up and down all day long. Sometimes we wore helmets, but not often. Inevitably, someone's bike would break down, and we would fight for turns on the only bikes left running. I would promise my brother, "Okay, one more trip up and down the driveway, and then you can have it. Really, *I promise!*" When I'd get back to the top of the driveway, my sweet brother was there waiting, all excited. I'd whip around and start down the driveway again. I had no intention of letting him ride my bike. I was such a selfish bully.

Colin, understandably fed up with my lies and deceit, cut me off at the turn, grabbed onto the handlebars, and tried to stop me. I was so *bad*. I gunned the accelerator and took poor Colin halfway down the hill, with him straddling the front of the bike, facing me, crying and screaming while the front wheel chewed up his ankles and I lost control, and we crashed. How awful I was! Colin would never have done that to me, a realization that gives me endless guilt now.

I was fast and fearless on motorcycles, and the pride I felt when I beat the boys knew no bounds. I crashed a lot! Once, while racing Roger's son Jordan up the driveway (after having been given strict orders not to), I got too close to the two-rail wooden fence and just couldn't get clear. The rail became a belt sander and carved out a good-sized dent in my outer thigh that is still there today. Another time I lost control and actually crashed through the fence and went bouncing down the steep hillside until I hit a tree. When I got up, the front shocks on my bike were bent, and blood was running down my leg where the foot peg had punctured the inside of my knee.

I remember trying to keep this from my mother, but my knee wouldn't stop bleeding. She found out and grounded me from riding for a whole week longer than my wound did. You see? That's why I had to hide these things from my mom. For one reason or another, I never got stitches and was left with a nice, deep hole in my knee.

There is a scene in *10* where Dudley Moore watches me rub suntan oil over my body—in slow motion, no less. Before we shot the scene, I went to the director, Blake Edwards, showed him my battle scars, and explained that we would have to shoot around them. Blake said, "Don't worry about it. I'll cut out your scars in the editing room." Blake had a funny little glint in his eye as he made his assurances. I should have known; Blake's sense of humor is legendary. When I saw the film for the first time, there was the hole in my leg, in a close-up *and* slow motion *and* blown up to about three feet across the screen.

The Collins kids from Torrance had the same problem every weekend at Ann-Margret and Roger's: trying to decide whether to play on the tennis court, the driveway, or in the pool. We were practicing our swan dives late one night when Roger came out and announced, "The astronauts are walking on the moon!" We all looked up at the big, fat moon, and my baby sister Kerry kept saying, "I can't see them!"

We were usually unsupervised. To this day, my parents don't know half the trouble we got into. Except the time we accidentally set Benedict Canyon on fire. One day, bored, with nothing to do, all seven of us decided to go camping. We took food—meaning marshmallows—blankets, tarpaulins for tent making and matches for lighting the campfire. A drawer in the Smiths' kitchen was always stocked full of assorted gum, which we raided all day. We brought some of the old paper gum wrappers to help us start the fire.

We spent most of the day building seven little camps, one for each of us. I was a serious Girl Scout and knew all about fires. We built lovely campfires out of pine needles and kindling, and started each of them with the blue gum wrappers. We stuffed ourselves on roasted marshmallows and got really hot, decided it was time for a swim, so we put out the fires, grabbed our gear, and headed back up the hill.

We were having a fine time playing in the pool when a big red fire engine came up the driveway. Tracy and I made the other kids swear not to say a word. "No matter what happens, don't say anything about our camps!" we demanded. I had taught my brother and sisters to lie well, so I felt secure they wouldn't spill.

Two firemen came up to the edge of the pool with our parents and interrogated us about the fire in the canyon. We all acted appropriately oblivious. "I don't know anything about a fire," I said. The other kids kept playing in the pool. Oh, they were good! Then one of the firemen held up a partially burned blue gum wrapper. Now, that would make most kids crack, but not us. Deny, deny, deny—that was our strategy. Until Roger started to work on our weakest link: his youngest, little Dallas.

"Come on, Dallas," he began. "You can tell me. If you tell me the truth, you won't get in trouble . . ."

Dallas broke into tears, and I knew then that we were doomed. He told everything.

My father was furious! He marched to the garage and came back with a boat paddle. We all had to line up and get out wet asses smacked hard with the paddle. All but Dallas.

Occasionally, Tracy and I would be invited into Ann-Margret's inner sanctum: her closet and bathroom. It was a beautiful and mysterious place to me. The floor was carpeted pink, and the sinks and counters were made of pink-and-white marble. There was a special sink just for washing your hair, like in the beauty salons.

My mother was always there. She and A-M had become best friends by then, just as Tracy and I were. My sisters were rarely invited in, although they wanted to be. But they were just little girls, and I wasn't sympathetic at all. I liked being special.

We would have long girl talks, and one day A-M said that she would be my godmother. Being raised in an agnostic home, I had heard the expression but didn't know what it meant. A-M explained that if anything ever happened to my parents, she would take care of me—she would take care of all of us. I remember thinking, *I wouldn't ever want anything to happen to my parents . . . but couldn't we just pretend for a little while? It would be so much fun.*

Some days A-M would give us beauty makeovers. We would start in her bathroom, where she let us play with her makeup. "Here, let me show you," she would say and take the eyeliner pencil from me. "Draw the line out just past the end of your lashes and then go up just a little at the corner," she said as she demonstrated on her own eyes. "This will make your eyes look bigger and a little catlike. Here, you try it."

Eventually, Tracy and I got pretty good at applying our makeup and learned all kinds of professional tricks of the trade from Ann-Margret. I still do my own makeup today when I do a photo shoot or a film. I'm impatient by nature and have a hard time sitting still for any length of time, so I get really annoyed when a makeup artist takes a long time, going over the same spot over and over again, or worse, gets carried away.

Hair was another story. Tracy and I both had the same blonde, superfine limp hair that was just too wispy to hold a style. After teasing and spraying for about an hour, Ann-Margret said, "You girls look better with the natural look. You should always wear your hair long and straight." I still do.

We would then make our way to her closet—or one of her closets, because Ann-Margret had three. One was for everyday clothes.

Even these were beautiful. I think the only sweats she has ever owned were made of cashmere. Her second closet was for her finer, evening wear. But we always went straight to the third closet, where she kept her glamorous Bob Mackie gowns and the glittering costumes from her nightclub shows.

We would all get giggle attacks and end up rolling around on the pink carpet, as A-M dressed us up in her gowns, feather boas and all. Now, Tracy was always more developed than I was; she was already curvy. She didn't fill out the gowns by any means, but she didn't swim in them like I did with my scrawny body. I always had long beach feet, though, so even at eleven years old I had no problem wearing Ann-Margret's tiny size 5 1/2 high heels.

Once Tracy and I were all properly gussied up, we would begin our victory walk, like beauty contestants, to show everyone how beautiful we were. We would go out to the pool where the other kids were playing. My sisters Kelly and Kerry were so sweet. They would look up at us in awe and tell us we were "so pretty!" The boys would always roar with laughter and scream, "I'm gonna barf!" as they did cannonballs off the diving board. Then we would traipse off to find my dad and Roger, who were usually in the garage, working on somebody's broken motorcycle. They would pretend to be so impressed and say nice things to us.

Ann-Margret would finish off our makeover by taking us to Scandia for lunch. Scandia was the ultimate Hollywood restaurant at the time, and her friends Bobby Darin or George Burns would stop by to say hello to A-M and to "admire" us. It must have been hard for them to keep a straight face. I know now that we looked completely ridiculous. But it was all very serious stuff to us at the time.

During school vacations, we would all go out to the Mojave Desert to ride motorcycles. The boys and the bikes would ride in Roger's big van, while the girls would ride in Ann-Margret's Rolls-

Royce. The boys would camp out in tents. Ann-Margret was fine with camping—as long as there was room service—so the girls would stay at the Holiday Inn in the town of Hesperia. I absolutely *loved* that hotel. I loved the maid service, the little soaps, the white towels that for some stupid reason I thought were cleaner than the ones we had at home. And the ice machine was just the coolest thing ever invented.

We kids would ride our bikes all day on the easy trails near where the van and the Rolls were parked. The adults would leave us on our own and take off for hours on the more challenging trails. But at some point in the day my father would ride in, drop off my mom, and take each of us for a ride. He always rode a big, deep rumbling motorcycle. For me, life didn't get any better than sitting behind my dad with my arms wrapped around him, his motorcycle going *vroom-vroom!* and vibrating under my behind. *Look at me!* I'd think proudly. *I'm riding with my dad!* He would go so fast! Up steep hills, the back wheel of the bike fishtailing in the loose dirt. He'd stick out his inside leg and skid around the sharp turns. "Hold on tight!" he'd warn. And I did, always confident that he would get us through an especially scary trail. He was my dad!

Late Sunday nights we went home to Torrance and to school. It wasn't a hard adjustment for us. I think we all felt so privileged to have escaped, even for a couple of days, the ordinary lives most kids lived. The other families in the neighborhood had conventional stay-at-home moms, and dads who left bright and early and returned home at five-thirty every night. Their menu for Monday night was always meat loaf, Tuesday was always fried chicken, Wednesday was always, etc., etc. Everything about their lives seemed routine, stable, reliable, clean, and neat. And, to us, *such* a bore. We were different, and very much aware of the criticisms and disapproval from the neighbors about how terrible it was that our parents left us alone so much. We were allowed to run around barefoot. And we got only a sympathetic *Tsk, tsk* at our eternally skinned knees, stubbed toes, smashed fingers, black eyes, and boxer cuts. Those were badges of honor, each scar a memento of a good time and a mark of a true Collins. It's a good thing there wasn't Child Protective Services then, or there would have been a nice little file on the Collins family.

Personally, I believe we were the luckier kids. We lived in a safe neighborhood. No child molesters—well, there was one teenage boy up the street who "diddled" with some of the dumber little girls. But we were too smart for him. No *way* he could talk any of us into his back bedroom!

While the neighbors snickered, my parents occasionally spent weekends with A-M and Roger, leaving us five dollars. A fortune! The first thing the four of us would do was to walk to the market for groceries, which meant macaroni and cheese or spaghetti. I let the most votes win on that decision. Then we would save thirty-five cents apiece for the movies, which is what it cost to go the Sunday matinee at the Stadium theater in downtown Torrance, four miles away, where we would usually see an old Elvis Presley movie. If it happened to be *Viva Las Vegas*, whenever Ann-Margret came on-screen, Kelly would tell the entire audience, "We know her. She's our friend." What was left of our five dollars went to dozens and dozens of penny candies.

The one rule my parents made absolute was that we could not see any of the neighborhood kids over the weekend. They weren't trying to hide anything, but they worried that kids who normally didn't enjoy the same degree of freedom (and with it, responsibility) as we did, might be more likely to get into trouble in a home with no parental supervision. This is the one rule I don't remember ever breaking.

My mother says that she would get a lump in her throat whenever she and my father drove away, but according to her, I was very mature for my age. She says, "I knew you could handle it." She knew, I think, because she saw so much of herself in me.

THREE

The world's past has been born on his back.
We are his heirs; he is our inheritance.

—ODE TO THE HORSE

I bred horses for twelve years. Horse breeding is one of the ways we humans try to play God. I decided which mare would be bred to which stallion, always having in my mind what the coupling might produce. This made me, the horse breeder, the creator of a living thing. Although I almost never got what I expected in a foal, I'm amazed at how many personality traits, mannerisms, and peculiarities are inherited. Horses aren't generally very distinct creatures, but when you get to know them very well, you begin to distinguish certain characteristics. Temperament, color, markings, and physical confirmation are most obvious. But even funny idiosyncrancies are passed down to the foal from the *dam* (the mother) and the *sire* (the father).

For instance, all of my stallion Centauro's foals inherited his unique way of tossing his head. It was a big, round double toss, as though he was drawing an imaginary double O in the air with his muzzle. He did it mostly when he was being especially showy and cocky, and always when he was being led out to breed a mare.

29

Another colt would have to shit in his water tank, just like his sire did. I've never figured out what that was about, but I understand it's not unheard of in the horse world. Novelist Jane Smiley even wrote about it in her book *Horse Heaven*. Another filly likes to drop a big mouthful of hay in her water, let it soak for a few minutes to make her own hay soup, then eat it when it has softened a bit, just like her dam.

Much has been made about environmental influences versus inherited influences. But most of these foals have never even *met* their sires. It's too dangerous. In the modern, unnatural setting of a breeding farm like mine, a stallion will often injure or even kill any horse that gets too close to a mare—including his own foal. Although humans are what I would call mutts (even royal families were never line-bred long enough to begin to compare with the generations of horses that have been documented), I'm still a confirmed believer in inherited behavior. It makes sense that so much of what makes me who I am was inherited in the same way.

If you ask my mother why she has such a sunny disposition, she'll tell you, "Because I got out of southern Illinois."

Her folks had a rough life there. My mother's mother, Elsie, was born on the family farm in southern Illinois, to poor, tough German immigrants. She was lucky to have gone to school through the third grade before she had to work on the farm or, as was common for little girls then, to be hired out as a cook on nearby farms.

At sixteen, Elsie, known to be the prettiest girl in town, went to work folding boxes at Owens-Illinois Glass Co. There she met my grandfather, Richard White—and soon got pregnant by him. The two of them married despite his English family's objections to the "pretty, dumb German girl." English-German enmity was strong after World War I.

Richard White's father, my great-grandfather, George, was a hardworking, hard-drinking man. He always wanted to be a soldier, but the U.S. military wouldn't have him, because of his clubfoot. So, around the turn of the century, he signed aboard a ship delivering mules to South Africa, where he planned to fight in the Boer War. Supposedly, the food and conditions aboard ship were so bad that George and the rest of the crew mutinied. As a result, he was arrested and thrown in prison upon his arrival in Cape Town. After three years, he escaped and stowed away on a ship bound for America.

He settled in an area of southern Illinois known as Little Egypt, because it resembled the delta of the Nile Valley. This region of Illinois was very corrupt and produced some of our most famous gangsters. Here, Great-grandfather George eventually found his calling as the distiller of the best sour mash in the county during Prohibition. He was arrested so many times that finally his daughter, my great-aunt Teen, pleaded with the local federal agent, "If you put it in the paper one more time that my dad was arrested, I'll never go to school again!" That wasn't the last time Great-grandpa was arrested, but it never made the paper again.

My grandfather built Elsie a three-room house in a predominantly black neighborhood on the outskirts of Alton, a town on the Mississippi River. The Great Depression had America in its grip, and for Elsie, having a house of her own must have been living high on the hog. My grandmother gave birth to her first daughter, Marjorie, and then my mother, Norma Jean. Shortly afterward, Grandfather Richard left for the Ozark Mountains to work on a dam project for the Works Progress Administration.

The workers all lived in tent camps. Elsie visited her husband only once. There is an old medical saying from the time: *One night with Venus, the rest of your life with Mercury.* Elsie came home with syphilis. As this was before the treatment penicillin was developed, she suffered from very gruesome and painful mercury injections.

When Richard returned from the Ozarks, he got a job at a lime quarry. The job required him to travel often, where he met and fell in love with another woman. He divorced Elsie, which was decent of him, considering divorce was uncommon in the 1930s; most women were usually abandoned. Grandfather moved to Baltimore and married his new love. But what makes him a really remarkable man for those days is that he always made his child support payments.

My grandfather died of lung cancer before I was born, probably as a result of his years spent working in the quarry. Who knows? Mom told me, "Those were the times. You didn't blame the lime or the company who owned the quarry. You were lucky to have a job." Her mother, Elsie, was fortunate to be able to return to Owens-

My grandmother, father, and mother, having fun—as usual.
PHOTOGRAPH BY DARLENE HAMMOND

Illinois Glass, where she folded boxes for another thirty years. I didn't know my grandmother very well. I saw her only a few times, and I remember being frightened of her because she was so quiet and stern!

While growing up, Mom and her sister Marjorie were alone most of the time, but they always had food, even if it was one scrawny chicken that they would make last a week. I have a photo of my mom in a tattered dress and shoes with big holes in them. "I was lucky," she tells me. "I had clothes and shoes. Lots of other kids didn't." Mom left home at sixteen and supported herself by teaching dance at various Arthur Murray dance studios.

The daredevil, happy-go-lucky, slightly nutty part of me probably comes from my father's side of the family. He says we are descended from Irish horse thieves. I suspect that my ancestors were really starving potato farmers, but, like Dad, I prefer the idea of horse thieves.

My paternal great-grandfather, Walter Collins, and my grandfather, Paul Collins, were quite a pair. They worked together in the coal mines of southern Illinois. Walter became mine superintendent during the formation of the United Mine Workers Union in 1890; the two of them caarried sidearms during this dangerous time. Paul was a mule driver in the mines. Part of his job description was to "clean up the mess" whenever the mules fell down the mine shaft. That meant getting another team of mules to pull out the dead ones. Wouldn't these two union men be turning in their graves to know that their progeny had all turned Republican!

Later, Great-grandfather Walter, a self-taught mechanic, built race cars. He was extremely successful with the "Collins Special," an undefeated dirt-track race car with a Fronty Ford engine. He raced all over Illinois, beating the likes of the Chevrolet brothers, and the famed team of Bender and Gaston, until his driver Sherman "Red" Campbell, was killed during a race in 1937. He then turned his mechanical talents to inventions and holds many engineering patents.

It's a creepy story about how both my great-grandfather and my grandfather died within hours of each other, in 1952. My father, Paul Collins (nicknamed P. C., to avoid confusion with his father), got a call from the hospital at about eleven o'clock one night, telling him that Walter had suffered what would turn out to be a fatal heart attack. Dad then called his father, told him what had happened, and said to wait until morning to go to the hospital, as it was 125 miles away. Paul, Sr., went anyway. After driving only ten miles, he veered off the unmarked road that was under construction and was killed.

My father had to tell his grandmother that her husband and only son were both dead. There was a ghastly double funeral—with open caskets—father and son laid out head to head.

My grandmother and namesake, Mary Collins, was born to a fine, respectable family. Her father was editor of the Benton, Illinois, newspaper. She too, became a journalist. In fact, Mary covered the 1928 execution of infamous gangster Charlie Birger, the last public hanging in the state. Grandmother passed away in 1999 at the age of ninety-two. Until the end, she remained independent, living alone and taking care of herself. I miss her terribly.

In the very early days of their marriage, my father had a Native American girlfriend named Two Star, who had been such a problem for my mother that she had their marriage annulled before I was born. When I asked Mom why she ever got back together with Dad, she said, "Your father was so much fun, I loved him, and he was going to California."

They never remarried, which makes the four of us kids bastards— a technicality I've always found exciting.

*   *   *

The friendship between my parents and the Smiths started to wane as the marriage between my mother and father began to die. Something serious happened during the filming of *C. C. and Company*, a film that Roger had written for Ann-Margret. It was about—what else?—motorcycles and costarred football great Joe Namath. I really don't need to know the details. I think parents should be able to have some privacy from their kids.

By now, my father had a new job as executive in charge of public relations and advertising for Hobie Cat, a superfun catamaran sailboat that had become his latest passion. What was it about my dad that he always ended up working for companies that made the toys he loved to play with? The timing of his new hobby and position was perfect for me. I was becoming discouraged from riding motorcycles because I had broken my leg when I crashed, once again, in a speed wobble. A speed wobble is a physics thing that happens when you're going too fast on uneven terrain. Your front end gets too light, and the wheel begins to wobble violently. There is an easy remedy to this problem: just gun the accelerator, and everything will straighten out. But we never got lessons about such things; we always learned by doing. Well . . . I learned about a speed wobble when I *de*celerated. The wobble got worse until I lost control, my bike and my body flip-flopped around and my world went black.

My brother, Colin, roused me from unconsciousness. He had been riding alongside me and saw the whole crash, and he looked so scared and concerned for me. My mouth was stuffed full of dirt. He helped me to my feet. When I stepped down on my right leg, I had no pain—yet—but something was wrong.

"Your foot is hanging kind of funny," said Colin. "Look, it's going the wrong way!"

There was no use even thinking that I could hide this one from my mom. My ankle was shattered and required surgery. The worst part for me was that the crash happened on the first Saturday of summer vacation. I was thirteen, and it really made me reevaluate my recklessness—at least for a little while.

I was on crutches and my leg was in a full cast from my big toe to the top of my thigh, but that didn't stop my father from teaching me to sail that summer. He just wrapped the cast in a trash bag, suspended it from the boom with the jib sheet, and headed out into the waves. I took to sailing the same way I took to motorcycle riding. I was pretty good, and very daring, and was saved by the U.S. Coast Guard countless times. Since we weren't going to the Smiths' house anymore, our weekends were spent going to sailing regattas all over the United States. We had to be there; it was part of Dad's job!

I remember my father being gone from home more and more. We kids were told it was because of Dad's business, but I knew better. My mother had begun to confide in me that my father had a girlfriend. I remember how upset she would get, sitting in bed and crying. She tells me now that I was a big comfort to her; that I was understanding and a good listener. I just recall being scared and not knowing what to say to her.

Mom bought lots of sheets and towels during this time. That was her way. When things got really bad, when she just had to get out of the house and away from facing us, her four little responsibilities, she used to tell me, "Watch the kids; I'm going out." She'd be gone a few hours and come back with big sacks of towels and bedding in bright, happy colors. They cheered her up.

One night while we kids were all spread out over the beanbag chairs my mother had made, and fighting over what to watch on TV, my father came in and turned off the TV. "Your mother wanted me to come tell you," he began. "I love you, but I won't be living here anymore."

I don't remember him saying much more. I think it was hard for him to say even that much. He was never good at serious, fatherly moments; he'd always left most of the parenting to my mother. Then he walked out the door, just like that. It wasn't such a shock to me, but it's still alarming when something like that actually happens. Colin, Kerry, and Kelly were confused and didn't understand any of it. My mother was out of commission, planted in her bedroom, curtains drawn. She didn't come out for days.

I gathered the kids together and explained that Dad wasn't coming home ever again. "He loves us," I tried to assure them. "As soon as he gets settled, we'll go see him. Everything's going to be okay, but you have to be really good now, because mom is not feeling good. She's sick, and we can't bother her." They started to cry. The poor little guys didn't understand why this was happening. They felt totally abandoned. I was surprisingly sensible about the whole drama. I think I was so totally secure in my father's love that I believed him when he said that we would see him soon. I knew his girlfriend, Carol, who was also his secretary. She had always been nice to us, and I instinctively sensed that Mom would be happier with Dad gone. And the selfish side of me thought, *Dad's moving to a beach house!*

Over the next few days, I took care of everything: getting the kids off to school, cooking, and so forth. I didn't do it to do a good deed or make myself look good. It was just the natural thing to do. We kids were an independent, well-working little unit.

On the fourth day of my mother's seclusion, Ann-Margret called.

I answered the phone. "Mom can't come to the phone, she doesn't feel well," I said.

"Don't tell your mom, but I'm coming over," said A-M.

When she arrived, she gave us each a big kiss on the cheek.

"Cathy, why don't you take the kids out for a couple of hours?" she told me.

I don't know what Ann-Margret said to my mom, but when we got home, A-M was gone, and Mom was in the kitchen, out of her funk for the time being. As she prepared one of our favorite dinners, tuna and potato-chip casserole (a southern Illinois staple), Mom told me that she was going to go to work for Ann-Margret as her personal assistant/girl Friday. I believe it was a good arrangement for everyone. A-M and my mother were already intimate friends, making it comfortable for A-M to have her around. Besides, my mother is extremely easygoing. But there was work for her only when A-M was making a film or playing Vegas. In between, Mom worked as a saleswoman at Bullocks department store in Torrance.

It's tempting for me to tell a sob story about how tough times were and how we had to wear hand-me-downs. But, nah, it would never hold up. Still, when A-M would clean out her three closets, Mom would come home with her car stuffed to overflowing. The clothes were beautiful—maybe a little over-the-top for the Torrance public schools, but little girls love to dress up.

One day, Mom drove Roger's van home with a new bed in back for me. It was round, with a big pink seashell-shaped headboard. Elvis Presley had given it to Ann-Margret during the filming of 1964's *Viva Las Vegas* and their famous romance (before she met Roger).

When I turned sixteen, A-M gave me freedom and independence by giving me her first car, a 1965 salmon-pink Ford Falcon convertible. I drove and drove that car, top up, top down, with no place in particular to go. I might drive to the store for a Coke—or to Tijuana to see the bullfights with my dad. Or to take my brother and sisters to the movies or any other place they wanted to go. I just *loved* to drive that pink convertible.

Only now can I imagine what a scary time it must have been for my mother. She was thirty-eight with four kids, no professional skills, and a soon-to-be ex-husband, who, while lots of fun, was, well, a carefree man. On top of all that, A-M was trying to have a baby. Mom was not the nanny type, so she knew she would soon be out of a job. She decided to take advantage of the hair and makeup skills she was learning by watching backstage. She entered a cosmetology school in Torrance to get her license, with hopes of eventually getting into the beautician's union.

A-M and Roger were supportive of Mom's decision; they even helped her financially while she went to school. But school took Mom a little longer than expected, because A-M never got pregnant. I know she tried so hard.

Mom's education was often interrupted by working Las Vegas with A-M. It was wonderful for us kids. We enjoyed the good life in the four-bedroom penthouse of the Las Vegas Hilton. We dined on room service most of the time and could charge anything in the hotel to Ann-Margret's suite, and hung out with A-M's dancers.

We didn't get into too much trouble, except for playing ding dong ditch in the hallways. And overstepping our privileges when we charged lunch to A-M's penthouse for the dozens of new friends we always made by the pool.

One night when I was just sixteen, an agent friend of Ann-Margret's approached me backstage and, I swear to God, said, "You ought to be in pictures." Sounded like a fine idea to me! I told him that I had done a little modeling and that I had just won a Miss Teen California beauty pageant—wisely neglecting to add that I'd been uncrowned after only two months because I refused to go to any more tiresome sponsors luncheons.

The agent's name was Kevin Casselman. I met with him again when I got back home. One of the first things he said was that I needed a new name. I was okay with that; I wasn't crazy about Cathy anyway. He said my name should be "Christina Collins." Christie wasn't much better than Cathy, in my opinion, but who was I to argue with him? He enrolled me in acting lessons with a respected teacher on Santa Monica Boulevard.

I tried my best at acting, I really did. I got onstage in front of the whole class and did my scenes like a good girl. I sang songs a cappella. I even participated in amateur psychotherapy and analyzed, along with the rest of the class, why I was all messed up. I still don't know why we had to do this so many times. Everybody's reason for his or her dysfunction was always the same: it was our parents' fault.

The classes were excruciating, but I hung in there until one night when we were to do rhythm exercises. A thin, strung-out looking actress, with big parent issues eagerly volunteered to go first. She went onstage and started to repeat some senseless sound over and over again. She got all wound-up, cried, and screamed like a banshee, and started banging her head against the wall—pretty hard, too. Everyone broke into wild applause! I got spooked, and I never went back to acting lessons again.

Kevin kept me busy auditioning, but I never even came close to landing a part. And the acting lessons and the gas, even at twenty-five cents a gallon for self-serve, were expensive. I had a job working the deep fryers at a fish-and-chips place on the pier in Long Beach. Modeling, at thirty dollars an hour, helped, though it was infrequent.

Somehow, my siblings and I were all saved from the alcoholism that ran in both sides of our family. I dabbled with drugs for only about four months, mostly pot and psychedelics. It's hard to believe now that I would ditch school and hitchhike, sometimes with friends and sometimes *alone*, down the Pacific Coast Highway to Hermosa

Beach. I'd meet up with other delinquents and bodysurf all day long, then hitchhike back to school and take the bus home. I finally got caught when I skipped school every day for a month. My mother was so mad, so disappointed in me, and insanely angry about all the mornings she'd gotten up early to drive me to school when I'd missed the bus. Her sleep was so important to her because she never got enough of it when she was working nights in Vegas with Ann-Margret.

By the time I got caught, I really was ready and relieved to be going back to school. Probably the best thing for someone like me is to be unsupervised and have the freedom to indulge in rebellious behavior. I got so bored with it!

FOUR

**It is the difficult horses
that have the most to give you.**

—LENDON GRAY

I met John Derek when was I sixteen years old.

I was at home one afternoon when my agent called. Kevin said that he wanted me to come into the office the next day to meet a director. "It has to be late in the day, because I'm going to school again," I said.

"Fine," he said and gave me the details about the film.

When I hung up the phone, Mom asked, "What's that?"

"I have an interview for a film that's going to be shot in Greece!" I was excited about the idea of going to Greece. I hadn't yet had enough rejection in Hollywood to be discouraged. In my mind, I was already scuba diving in the Aegean.

Mom asked, "Who's making it?"

I read from my notes. "His name is . . . John Derek."

Mom suddenly got excited.

"Oh my God, John Derek!" she exclaimed.

"Who's John Derek?" I asked.

"He's so *handsome!* He was one of my favorite actors, and now he's a photographer and a director. His hair is silver now, and he's even more handsome!"

43

Mom went with me to the meeting. We were waiting in the office when he came in. She was right: he was *so handsome*. I'd never seen a more beautiful man. He was darkly tan, which set off his green eyes and silver mane of hair that looked as though the wind had blown it back, perfectly messy. He was wearing white jeans and a white denim shirt that were both soft and old, almost threadbare, and frayed in all the right places.

Yet there was no pitter-patter in my heart; no love at first sight. For me, John's looks were just something to be enjoyed; he was so very easy to look at. Mom, on the other hand, seemed a little giddy.

I don't recall much of the meeting. I was ridiculously shy; probably didn't say two words beyond "Yes," "No," "Thank you." But I do remember John saying that I was completely *wrong* for the part. The character was Greek, and my long blonde hair was a big problem. I said that I wouldn't mind dyeing it. (Remember: *I wanted to go to Greece!*) So it was arranged that he would come photograph me in a couple of days.

John told me later that as he was driving to my house, deeper and deeper into the marginal part of the L.A. suburbs, he was sure that the directions Kevin had given him were wrong. He said he just couldn't believe that the girl he'd met in the office lived in this neighborhood. That girl was too sophisticated, he'd thought.

He shot some pictures of me in our backyard. For some reason, most of the yard was filled with a big green tent. John shot with very long lenses, which put him far away, even while shooting close-ups. The distance was nice for me, being so nervous. He was very pleasant, but I couldn't read whether or not he was happy with the session. After the first roll of film, John said that he would really like to take some more pictures up at his house, where he had the proper lighting equipment, and where his wife, Linda, could help him.

"Linda" was Linda Evans. I was a big fan from watching her, and the big buckskin horse, on the 1960s television series *The Big Valley*.

The next day I drove to John's house in my pink convertible. Linda opened the door and greeted me with such warmth and sheer beauty, I could hardly meet her eyes. She was wearing very short shorts and a faded once-red sweatshirt that was cut off at the neck and the sleeves. She just looked unbelievable to me.

The house was fabulous. Very masculine, with lots of exotic furs and lovely oversized antiques. A big waterfall that John had built came rushing down the hillside, through big boulders just outside a wall-sized window.

Linda asked, "Cathy [Christina never stuck], would you like something to drink?"

"Yes," I said while finding a big fur-covered floor pillow to sit on.

As Linda went to the kitchen, John looked at me and said, "Don't you say please or thank you? Linda has better things to do than to get you a Coke!"

God, I wanted to die. I didn't mean to be rude, I was just so timid and nervous, I could hardly say anything at all. Of course, none of this came out of my mouth. I barely managed a tiny "Sorry."

Now that the day was off to a bad start, John led me to another room. As I entered, I saw a big wall covered with *my face!* The photograph took my breath away. Not that I enjoyed seeing myself enlarged to four by six feet. But the photograph was beautiful. The face was mine, yet not mine, and it wasn't trick photography. I didn't even have on a speck of makeup. I stood there while John put up another dozen photographs of me on the wall. Finally he said, "Don't you like them?"

"Yes," I said, but my head was screaming, *You'd better say more than that! Time to get over your shyness right here and now!*

"They're beautiful!" I finally mustered.

That seemed to be enough. I later learned that John was accustomed to strange reactions to his photography. Raquel Welch once sat as silently as I had until about the eleventh photograph before screaming for John to stop. Then she stared at one photo of herself for about ten minutes, mesmerized.

John went through the photos once more, telling me what he liked, what he didn't like, what he wanted to get more of, and what he definitely wanted to eliminate. He put up one such photo and observed, "See, here you look like you're smelling shit."

I nodded, although I had always thought that the pose in question was one of my sophisticated expressions that I had learned from modeling. But when he put it the way he did, I saw immediately what John was seeing, and I had to admit that he was right.

He put up another. "Now, here your mouth is pursed and tight, like a chicken's asshole!"

Boy, he was blunt. But he was right again. I instantly recognized that tight mouth as my grandmother's. It was an expression of hers that the whole family found irritating and annoying.

He came over, took me to a window, put a second set of glasses on top of the ones he was already wearing, and stared at me hard in the bright light. "Good, your face is clean, no makeup," he said. "Let's go to work."

We went upstairs to the pool, where Linda was setting up lights. We started to shoot some photos with me sitting under a tree. I was wearing jeans and a pretty blue blouse with little yellow flowers. Ann-Margret had given it to me. After several rolls of film, John asked if I would go in the pool and shoot some with my hair wet.

Linda took me down to her closet, where she found a blue crocheted bikini that she could make smaller for me by tightening the strings at the hips. Linda was so sweet to me. I don't think she took my earlier brevity to be rude; I think she sensed my shyness. Once I was in Linda's bikini, we both went back to the pool.

John told me later that Linda, who was walking behind me as we came up the stairs, had given him a thumbs-up about my body. Over the years, John had photographed so many beautiful girls, or girls who *thought* they were beautiful, only to discover that they were the result of tons of makeup or hideous plastic surgery. Many of the girls expected John to be able to "fix" their imperfections with his camera. He hated being put in that position. He'd say, "I'm not a magician. I make women look beautiful, because I shoot beautiful women! I can't make a silk purse out of a sow's ear."

He was being modest. I truly believe that he saw light and shadow and color more vividly than other people. Probably the way you see things when you are on certain drugs, as when I took LSD. Things appear more rich and intense. John just had an eye. That doesn't mean that being photographed by him was fun. It wasn't. He was not like the stereotypical photographer straight out of central casting you see in the movies: "Hold it right there! Oh, that's beautiful! Oh, yeah, baby, just like that!" Feigning some kind of orgasmic pleasure that's supposed to give you confidence. They're so full of shit.

John was different; very impatient and outspoken. You'd more likely hear: "Relax your mouth! Move your chin just a little! I said just a *little*, not a whole fucking mile! Look happy, for Christ's sake!" Or, as he said to beautiful Shania Twain the first time he photographed her: "Somebody get me a knife. I've got a gorgeous shot here, but I've got to cut that bump off her nose!"

Once you got over the initial shock, there was something about John's bluntness that could create magic. For those girls who didn't run home in tears—and some did—they started to relax and discard the false smiles and comely expressions learned from childhood. They became beautiful and serene, almost emanating a special, glowing loveliness from within. I saw it happen so many times.

While showing me the photos from our shoot in the pool, John said that he wanted me for the film. But he stressed that I would have to work very hard. I would have to start rehearsals right away and immediately dye my hair dark. Dying my hair meant nothing to me, and, sure, I could work hard. I had no fear of acting or being able to carry the lead in a film. That was John's problem. I was going to Greece!

John sent me to Jon Peters to have my hair dyed a beautiful dark shade called titian. Jon was only a famous Beverly Hills hairdresser then, not yet the boyfriend of Barbra Striesand or the head of Columbia-Sony Pictures. (Only in Hollywood!) At the time, my hair had a slight green tint to it—because I was taking scuba-diving lessons in a swimming pool suffering from chemical imbalance. "No problem," said Jon. "I've got a product made just for this."

When he rinsed off the product in the shampoo bowl, I could see in his eyes that something had gone wrong. I pushed him away and said, "Let me see!" I looked in the mirror and burst into tears. My hair was *carrot orange*. Jon just laughed and swept me into his arms. He carried me all over his salon, kissing my cheek and saying, "Don't worry, it's going to be all right. Oh, please stop crying!" I finally did stop and went home with orange hair. Jon was never able to get it anywhere near a natural color, so Mom finally sent me to a hair-dresser friend of hers who made my hair a beautiful dark brown. I loved being a brunette, and I liked the way I was treated. Blondes might have more fun, but blondes also have the image of being intellectual lightweights.

With the drama of my hair over, I started rehearsals at John's house with the actor who was to play the male lead in the film. I hated rehearsals. I felt like such an idiot, doing pantomimes and improvisations, reciting Shakespeare. The actor loved it, though; he was in heaven.

The film got delayed for two months because of financial problems, and I caught a serious case of disinterest. Hard work is fine, as long as it doesn't go on forever, which is what this felt like to me at sixteen. I take after my father in that we get bored very quickly and move on. I was getting lazy and not doing much more than showing up for rehearsal. At this point in my life, I'd never had to stick with something or even been forced to be disciplined. John was getting frustrated—and told me so. He said that he wanted to fire me, but Linda had talked him out of it. "The girl is young, John. She is perfect for your film, and she's a good girl," she told him. "Be patient with her."

One day I confessed to John, "I'm bored."

"Bored people are boring," he said.

Such a simple combination of a few words, but the little bell in my head rang. The statement seemed so true. I've never been bored since.

John told me that I was lazy, getting fat, and obviously not ready for the responsibility required to star in a film. He said that we should both think about things over the weekend. I was a bit shell-shocked. I'd never been fired before. My mother and I drove to Ann-Margret's house to help her pack for Vegas. While we were sitting on her bed, I told A-M what had happened. She was very serious with me. "This is a big decision for you," she said. "If you go ahead with the film, you must commit yourself completely."

"But I hate him," I said, meaning John. "He's mean. He picks on me. He says I'm lazy."

A-M knew me well and probably suspected that John was right. "You must respect your director, do whatever he says, and turn yourself over to him," she told me. "He is the captain of the ship."

If she had only known where her advice would lead me.

FIVE

Far back, far back in our dark soul,
the horse prances.

—D. H. LAWRENCE

With Linda's intervention, John and I mended our fences, and in November 1973, my mother and I joined John, Linda, a pack of actors, and a sizable crew on the Greek island of Mykonos to make the movie *Once upon a Time*. It wasn't my first time out of the U.S.; my father had taken me with him on a business trip to the Orient when I was thirteen. But I especially loved being on a tourist island in the off-season. We were the only foreigners there for almost three months. I got to know all the local fishermen and the knitting women who made sweaters for the next year's invasion of tourists. A revolution in Athens put the whole country on curfew—except for our little island.

In this lovely atmosphere, my mother began a sweet romance with a handsome Greek. It's a wonderful thing to see your mother, whom you naturally assume has entered into a sexless existence at the old age of forty, reveling in a man's attention. My mother, who had become a hard-working, serious, tired single mother of four, was suddenly transformed into a feminine, vital young woman.

As I would be eating breakfast with the crew to begin my work-day, Mom would come through, give me a kiss on the cheek, and cheerfully say good morning to us all before going upstairs to her room. At about the time we would be leaving for the set, Mom would come back through, showered and changed, ready to begin another day and night on Dimitri's yacht or maybe a road trip to the other side of the island.

John and I were getting along pretty well. I didn't hate him any-more, but I can't say that he was my favorite person in the world. But he seemed happy enough with what I was doing in the film. About four weeks into shooting, Linda went back to the States to work on a television movie. She was only gone about a week when something happened.

Something serious.

I'm not being coy when I say something *happened*. There was no flirting, no lingering looks, none of the normal behaviors that begin a romance. John and I started spending more time together when Linda left, but I didn't think anything of it. No one did. She would be back in ten days, and everyone in the world knew that the Dereks were the world's happiest, most loving couple. John and I would go to dinner after shooting and talk, talk, talk. Well, actually, I would listen most of the time. Unless the conversation turned to surfing or sailing, I couldn't contribute much. He spoke about life and death and history and the state of the world. I listened and listened and listened.

For my seventeenth birthday, the cast and crew threw me a party that ended with all of us drinking ouzo and throwing our glasses, dishes, and a couple of chairs into the fireplace. John gave me a gold chain bearing a little sea sponge wrapped in a gold cage. He'd had it made for me. He said that I should wear it around my neck, and always remember to be a sponge in life and absorb as much knowl-edge as I could.

One night, while mom was with Dimitri, and Linda was still in L.A., John and I were walking back to the hotel through the narrow streets of Mykonos. The maze of passages had been designed to confuse attacking pirates. John stopped in front of one of the island's 365 churches—one for every day of the year—and kissed me. It was soft and sweet and simple. I don't remember being shocked. I don't remember thinking anything at all; I just enjoyed it.

I should have heard bells and warning sirens go off in my head, telling me to stop. I should have thought, *This is wrong. He's married. He loves Linda.* You *love Linda.* All these thoughts would come later. For that moment, kissing John just seemed the right thing to do.

My mother had given me a journal before we left for Greece. She said that I was going off on a once-in-a-lifetime adventure and that one day I might want to look back and read what this great opportunity was like for me. I was a good girl and followed her advice, writing in my journal every night. One day, many days after the kiss, I came home from the set and found my mother sitting in my room with my open journal in her hands. She was crying.

"What are you doing?" I asked.

She stood up and slapped me across the face. "How could you do this?" she screamed. "He's married!"

Blood spurted from my nose, lots and lots of blood, like turning on a tap. It wasn't as bad as it looked. I had grown up having nosebleeds all my life; it's just the way I'm built. I ran out of the room and down the outdoor hallway. John came out of his room and looked shocked as I ran up to him with blood gushing down the front of my shirt.

"What the hell happened?" he said. I grabbed a towel from his bathroom, held it to my nose, and laid down on the floor. I am an expert at nosebleeds.

"My mother read my journal, and she knows," I blurted.

"But why are you bleeding?"

By then, I was gagging on the blood running down the back of my throat. John was starting to look pale. "I'm okay, really," I said. "It's just a nosebleed. I get them all the time."

He wasn't completely convinced. As I was later to learn, the sight of blood tended to make John grow faint—an aftereffect of his service in the Philippines during World War II.

"I'm going to go talk to your mother," he said.

He found her in the hallway, just as she was coming out of my room.

"Get away from me, John Derek!" she screamed.

"Let's talk about this, Norma," he said calmly.

She started to back up into my room. John reached out to try to settle her, but she was hysterical and combative.

"Don't you touch me!" I could hear her scream.

They began a pathetic dance around the bed, with John trying to soothe her and my mother screaming, "Fuck you, John Derek! Fuck you!"

I don't think I'd ever heard my mother say *fuck* before. But as I have learned, in certain situations it's the only word that will do. She was a wounded bearcat, insane with anger at John, but more at me. And I don't blame her. I must have hurt her very much. The fact that her daughter was involved in possibly breaking up a marriage must have been so hard for her to accept. After all that she had gone through with my father, she was ashamed of me.

John came back to his room at about the same time I was getting up off the floor. The bleeding slowed to a managable trickle.

"You'd better go stay with your mother," he said. "We'd better not see each other for a while. Linda gets back in a few days, and I have to think."

When I walked back into my room, Mom said she was disgusted with me and left. I tore up my journal, never to have another.

The next days of filming made for a strange situation. John directed me as the actress in his film, but there was nothing else. No eye contact, except what couldn't be avoided.

Linda came back, and I could tell by her demeanor that John had told her everything. I saw her just a couple of times, and only because I couldn't evade her completely. She was always very proud and dignified, making me feel even more awkward and ugly.

On Christmas Day, the cast and crew arranged to go to the tiny island of Delos, about an hour's boat ride from Mykonos. I was sitting at the bow of the boat with my mother and the script girl when I heard a small prop plane buzz overhead. I looked up and knew it was Linda. For no good reason, I had this powerful conviction that she was leaving. I got a sick feeling in my stomach.

Oh God, what have I done? I thought, then did my best to put it out of my mind, at least for the day.

Delos is a barren little island that hasn't been inhabited for hundreds of years. There was a pier for docking our chartered boat; one restaurant for tourists, and it was closed for the season; and ruins and temples dedicated to the Greek gods. As we broke off into little groups to explore Delos, I withdrew into my thoughts and tried to make sense of what was happening. I was involved in something that seemed to have a pace of its own. It was going faster than I was, and I didn't seem to be able to keep up with it. In one respect, walking around the ruins of homes where people lived over a thousand years ago made my problems seem silly and insignificant. But at the same time, I had a spooky feeling that I was in trouble.

I never thought that Linda would leave or that John would let her. Never. I just knew with my whole being that when she returned,

John and Linda would be together again. I loved John, yes. Looking back, I loved him as much as a seventeen-year-old girl could love a man. I wasn't a virgin when I met John, but that was a mere technicality. At sixteen I'd realized that I was the only virgin among my friends. So I quickly found an obliging boy and joined their ranks. But the event itself was meaningless. I wanted to be near John, spend all my time with him—in the present. But that was a horrendous reason to meddle in a marriage. My feelings weren't complicated by thoughts of the future or commitment, and (obviously) not complicated enough by what was right or wrong.

When we all got back from Delos, I declined Christmas dinner and went to my room. The group was too joyous for me. I needed a good cry. By the time I was into it good and heavy, John came to my door. He didn't look much better than I did. He said that Linda had gone back to the States. They had talked and fought it out until Linda decided to leave, to let him get to know "the girl, get her out of your system." She believed that it was just a matter of time before the infatuation would die out, and that John would soon look at me and see only a vapid surfer girl. *She's right,* I thought.

He asked me if I would go with him to Germany for the film's postproduction. No promises, he said. "See what happens." I could have—should have—said no. But I didn't; I wanted to be near him.

When I told my mother that I was going to Germany with John, she absolutely refused. She told me that she had my passport and that I was going to go home with her as soon as the film was finished. We talked for a long time, and we both cried a little. "This can't work, you know," she told me. "I don't want you to get hurt."

"Mom, it's too late for that," I said. "I love him."

She went to her closet, pulled out my passport from where she had hidden it, and handed it to me. "You should call your father and tell him," she said.

I did. "Dad. . . ." I began. And then I paused. How do you tell your father that you're in love with a man older than *he* is, and you want to go live with him in Europe? "Dad . . . I've gotten involved with John."

My father's reaction was bewildering.

"I know. Your mother told me," he said, his voice very gentle.

"Um . . . I want to go to Germany with him. For a while."

There was a long pause. "Well," he said at last, "I've always told you to do what feels right for you; to do what makes you happy. And if this is what you really want to do, then it's okay with me."

"*Oh,*" I said, meaningfully.

Then he said something that stunned me. "But I want to know that you really know what you're doing," he said. "At some point I want you to come home so that I can look into your eyes and see that you are happy."

What a sweet, lovely—but shocking—thing to hear my father say. Dad was fun, and I never questioned his love for me, but he had never been sentimental that way, at least not that I could remember. He hadn't even been particularly fatherly.

"Sure, Dad, I will, soon," I said.

"I love you," he said.

"I love you too."

I suppose my parents' semiblessing came from their own life experiences. They had both left home when they were sixteen; not to travel Europe with a lover, but to leave the nest and begin their own life adventure. Although they were afraid for me, I think they recognized that I was on my way to an exciting adventure of my own—albeit, most likely a painful one. And as my mother says now, "I always knew that you were capable. If you wanted to, you could find your way back home."

Probably the happiest times of my early love affair with John was the last week of filming in Greece. We still had much work to do, and the anticipation of playing house with him left me anxious but light-hearted most of the time. At the end of the week's shoot, the whole cast and crew took a ferry to Athens to catch our respective planes. A huge storm turned an eight hour trip into twenty-two. Although I was basically brought up on the sea, I have a serious problem with seasickness. I inherited it from my father. We even had our own dive boat, but unless he was skippering, he got deathly ill. Most of the Collins kids spent at least half the forty-five-minute trip to Catalina Island feeling seasick.

On arrival at Emerald Bay, my father's remedy would be to get us into our wetsuits and throw us into the water. I say *throw us* because getting into a wetsuit was the last thing we wanted to do. It was a pain in the ass to get into a wetsuit back then. They didn't have the pretty colored slippery linings that wetsuits have now. These were formfitting inner tubes. I hated my wetsuit, and I didn't care if we were the second kids in the world to have them, as my father claimed. He had paid a fortune for them, and we were going to use them. I still get nauseous when I smell baby powder, overcome by my association of being in the boat anchored in a cove, rocking with the slow swells of the ocean. I always wanted to puke while my mother dusted the vile black rubber straightjackets with baby powder, and then tried to pull them onto our uncooperative little bodies, like O. J. trying on the glove.

Our "perfect storm" in Greece hit in the afternoon. After the first hour, we were given life vests and blankets and told to get under the tables in the dining room. That's when I ran to the bathroom. The ladies' room was disgustingly filthy, but soon I was wrapped around the toilet, hanging on for dear life while the waves slammed the ship around. I got so sick! I remember getting such pleasure from the slimy floor because it was so cool to my cheek. My fingernails were imbedded with the black grime that came off the floor when I scratched to grab hold of something when the boat rolled *way* too far to starboard. I didn't come out until we docked in Athens. In the port, John told me that when he was going over to the Philippines on a troopship, two of the men jumped overboard because they couldn't handle their seasickness. This made me want to hurl all over again.

Saying good-bye to Mom at the airport was so sad. She was worried about me, sure that she was making a big mistake. I could see in her eyes that she might change her mind any second and take me home with her. John kissed her on the cheek and promised to take care of me.

My first night with John was spent outside of Munich in the beautiful old Hotelschloss, which sits next to a centuries-old castle. We would be faithful to each other for the next twenty-five years.

We quickly got into our "off-to-work-we-go" routine, taking a streetcar to Studio Bavaria, where John was finishing the film. I loved postproduction and learned the technical side of it rapidly. It turned out that I have good problem-solving skills in editing, and my ear for sound is quite good. I was soon put to good use as an assistant to the assistant to the editor.

At the end of the workday we would head back to our castle hotel. All was fine for the first couple of weeks, then everything started to go dark. John was becoming gloomy. And, being John, he was completely honest with me.

"What the fuck have I done?" he would say. "I love Linda. How could I hurt her like this? I'm such a prick! I deceived her and cheated on her."

Here it comes, I'd think to myself. *He's come to his senses, and he's going to send me home.*

"But you didn't cheat on her," I said.

"Sex isn't the only act that constitutes cheating," he said. "I'd rather my lover have sex with someone than a long, intimate conversation. I should have told her the second I became interested in you. That was our deal."

I just stared at him and started to cry.

I couldn't think of anything to say. I tried to stop crying and managed to look at him blankly.

He looked into my eyes. "I know there's something in there," he said. "Say something, for Christ's sake!"

Poor John. He was so sure that any day I would blossom into an exciting, young spirit. That's usually what an older man gets when he falls in love with a young girl. I suppose I eventually did grow into myself, whatever that is, but I was a slow grower for a long time.

Finally, I said, "I don't want to go home," then began crying again. "I want to stay with you."

Our days together grew increasingly dismal, with very little that was pleasurable. One night the phone rang. I thought, *Oh, no, it's Linda.* Again, for no good reason, I knew it was her. This was the second of many uncanny encounters I would have with Linda. John hated the phone, so answering it, in German, was my chore. I made some excuse why I couldn't pick it up. John did, and I could tell by his side of the conversation that he was uncomfortable but putting on a pleasant spin. He ended with "I love you," and hung up. He looked over at me and said, "That was Linda. She said that everything is fine at home. She asked if I was still happy with 'the girl.' I told her, 'I don't know.' "

As I suspected, in the morning John asked me to go home. "I've made a big mistake. I don't know what I'm doing anymore," he said. "I can't stand myself. I can't stand that she is waiting for me when I've been such a shit to her."

"All right," I said.

"Your father asked you to come home and look him in the eyes. I think this would be a good time," said John. "This is not good for you here. I just make you cry all the time."

I nodded and cried some more.

For some bizarre reason, John suggested that I see Venice before I went home. He thought everyone should see Venice. I wanted to see Venice, I really did, but now? He drove me there and proceeded to show me the most beautiful city ever built, where the light is like no other place in the world. He took some beautiful pictures of me along the canals, then put me on a plane home. He was a strange one.

I never got a chance to call home and warn my mom that I was coming. Her mouth gaped when I walked through the door and told her what had happened—that I was, in essence, "on standby" until further notice. Mom was sweet; she didn't make me feel like a fool. She said, "You should call your father."

It was the father I knew who answered the phone. "Hello," he said in his usual upbeat way.

"It's me," I said. "I'm back."

"Great, we're just leaving to go skiing," said Dad. "You want to go?"

"Sure," I said, thinking that the five-hour drive to Mammoth Mountain would give us ample time to talk; for him to *look into my eyes*, and all that.

He picked me up with Nancy, the woman who would turn out to be his future wife and the love of his life. I love Nancy. A pretty, petite brunette, she has the look my father has always found attractive. When my father and Nancy fell in love, it caused quite a scandal on Beach Road in San Juan Capistrano, because she was the wife of my father's boss.

Dad, Nancy, and I talked all the way to Mammoth, up in the mountains north of Los Angeles. Dad talked about his new job with Goodyear (no kidding, he would need a new job and a new boss now!) and how it required him to relocate to Texas. We talked about what I had seen in Greece, Germany, and Venice; we talked about everything except John. I wasn't going to bring it up until Dad did—which meant that we never talked about John. We had a great weekend skiing and lots of fun, but we never got serious, never did the "eye thing." That was my dad.

The ten days or so that I spent at home are a blur to me now. But I did have a little investigating to do. Mom told me that there were rumors going around that someone was trying to bring serious charges against John for statutory rape, contributing to the delinquency of a minor, and violating the Mann Act. She was sure that Dad wasn't behind this, so that left my agent, Kevin Casselman, as the most obvious suspect. I called Kevin.

"Thank God you're back!" he said. "You have to stay away from that man!"

"Why?" I asked.

"He's a Svengali," said Kevin.

"Huh?"

"A mesmerizer. A Pygmalion."

"A *what?*"

"A man who brainwashes women and uses them."

"If he's so bad, Kevin, then why did you work so hard to get me the part in the first place?" I asked finally.

"You're right, I shouldn't have," he said. "I'm warning you now. He'll ruin your career just like he did to Ursula and Linda!" Ursula being the gorgeous Swiss actress Ursula Andress, John's second wife.

"What career?" I said. "I have no career!"

"You're going to be a big star, I'm telling you, and he'd better keep away from you." Kevin was frantic now.

"Calm down, Kevin," I said. "I'm not sure I even want to be in the picture business. You haven't seen the film, and I didn't really enjoy acting very much."

Kevin started screaming, "You ungrateful little bitch! After all that I've done for you? I won't let this happen!"

I was stunned. I'm tempted now to make up a clever, devastating retort, but in reality I said something like, "You leave me alone."

Unfortunately, my research turned up the fact that in California, anyone could file a complaint. It didn't have to be signed or confirmed by the parents. It was from an old Spanish law, whereby the child belongs to the state. Meaning John was screwed.

SIX

Ride a cockhorse to Branbury cross,
To see a fine lady upon a white horse:
Rings on her fingers and bells on her toes,
She shall have music wherever she goes.

—NURSERY RHYME

"John's on the phone," Mom called out. I ran, my heart beating in my throat.

"Calm down," she said.

"Right," I agreed. But the optimist in me was excited.

"Hi," I said meekly.

"Hi," said John. "I know I shouldn't be saying this. I know there's no future in it. But do you want to come back and see how long it lasts?"

"Yes. I'll be there as soon as I can get there." I took the first flight back to Germany. I knew there was no future in it, too, but "as long as it lasts" was good enough for me.

Our life in Germany picked up pretty much where we had left off. There was a lot of downtime now in the postproduction schedule, so we started traveling. We rented a little Peugeot station wagon and saw Europe. *All of it.* We would drive all day and sleep in little *pensiones* or scrunched up under a blanket in the back of the car. John was a superb guide. Ursula had shown him Europe some years before, then he had taken Linda there, so by the time it was *my* turn he knew it very well. Touring by car rarely required us to go through passport control. A good thing, because handing over our passports to immigration had become nerve-racking. My heart would pound in my ears as the agent would carefully look at John and his passport. Then he'd look me right in the eyes and scrutinize my passport. He'd check every stamp in it and then compare the numbers on a long Wanted list sitting on his desk. It was like a scene right out of the movie *Midnight Express*. I always wondered if, this time, Interpol would take John away to the pokey for "kidnapping" me.

I wanted a new name to go with the new me. I was still a brunette, and I didn't feel like a sunny southern California Cathy anymore. Cathy was a fine name for a blonde surfer girl, but not for the bohemian, adventurous me who was living in Europe with an older, sophisticated man. What irritated me most about my name was the way people seemed to put it up their nose when they said it. I tried my real name, Cathleen, for a while, but everyone still greeted me with the same cheerful "Hi, Cathy!" John was fine with the idea of me changing my name.

"Just make sure you like your new name," he said. "You'll be stuck with it. When the studio wanted to change mine, Harry Cohn said I could keep one of my names, and I chose to keep Darec. Cohn said, 'Fine. John Derek!' I said, 'A john's a toilet!' But I didn't fight him about it, and now I'm called a toilet for the rest of my life."

I tried on many names for size: uncute names like Roberta, Laura, Deborah. But those break down to Robbie, Lori, Debbie. I don't remember where "Bo" came from; probably a friend recommended it. No diminution for Bo. Can't make Bo cute. Can't say it through your nose, either. *Perfect!* I thought, and I have been Bo ever since.

The fact that John had left Linda for a teenybopper was truly disturbing to their friends back home. John and Linda were known as the perfect couple; people in L.A. saw them as proof that true love between two beautiful people could endure. John's conduct was messing with their sensibilities.

John Wayne called.

"Author!" he shouted into the phone. He liked John's writing and always called him Author. "What the hell are you doing, you stupid son of a bitch? Don't you know Linda is my favorite lady? She's the best thing that ever happened to you, and here you are going off with this little girl."

"I know, I know," John said.

"Is she beautiful?" asked John Wayne.

"Yes," John answered.

"I figured," said Duke. "You stupid son of a bitch."

One day, the phone rang and—*Uh-oh!*—I knew it was Linda calling again. She was calling to ask John if perhaps they should file for divorce. She said that if he was serious about "the girl," she wanted to start dating again, if it was okay with him. John gave her his blessing and said that he loved her.

John told me precisely what was bothering him: "If there was a way to ask her not to divorce or date, I would. We're not getting along very well, but that would make me a real prick, wouldn't it?"

Just then, *I swear,* Ursula called. I could hear her heavily accented voice over the phone.

"*Chon!*" she admonished him. "What are you doing with this girl? How could you do this to Linda?"

"Shit, Urs, I don't know," said John.

"Is she a good girl, Chon?"

"Yes, she's a good girl."

"I need you to sign some papers for me," said Urs.

"What kind of papers?" asked John.

"Oh, Chon," said Urs, "they're just some divorce papers."

"I don't know, Urs. Linda just called for a divorce, and I don't know if I can handle two in the same night."

"Chon!" Ursula exclaimed. "It's just a technicality. Switzerland doesn't acknowledge our Tijuana divorce!"

"Come on, Urs. Things aren't working out with the girl, and I've been thinking that maybe we should get back together . . ."

"*Ayeeee!*" I could hear Ursula screeching and laughing.

"We'll come to Switzerland for the weekend, and I'll sign your papers," said John. "I want you to meet the girl."

I was always *the girl*. The girl who broke up a beautiful marriage. People blamed John, because I was so young. But it wasn't completely his fault. At seventeen, I knew right from wrong, and I knew I was doing wrong. I could have stopped it but chose not to. It's an awesome, powerful feeling to know that a man has turned his life upside down for you, and sometimes I felt downright evil. I can take some comfort now in the fact that we were obviously meant to be together. If only someone had told us that we would be a couple for twenty-five years, maybe our first years together would have been happier. But of course no one could have predicted that. Knowing you are responsible for someone's pain is a terrible way to begin a relationship, and John wept from the guilt of hurting Linda. She was a dark cloud that hung over us for a long, long time.

We took the train to Bern, Switzerland, and Ursula picked us up at the station. She was exquisite, wearing a big fur coat the same color as her own long, tawny blonde hair. But it was those eyes lined in kohl, those yellow cat's-eyes, that bore right through me as we were introduced. I was aware that John and Ursula were still friends; their continuing relationship was well-known.

"I still love her as much as I ever did," John had told me. "We don't play house anymore, that's all."

How nice, I thought. But I was struck at seeing for myself their deep, genuine affection for each other. It was much more than a friendly politeness; it was free of any self-consciousness. They joked and laughed and truly appreciated each other.

As soon as we got to Urs's family home, John went over to the bright light by the window. He put on his double glasses and said to Ursula, "I haven't seen you in a while. Come over here."

"I will not!" Ursula said, putting her hands on her hips, looking like the goddess she typically played on-screen.

"Come on, Urs, let me see you," insisted John.

"Oh, Chon." Ursula sighed as she walked over to the window.

He took her chin in his hands and looked her over good. Urs peered up at him like a little child.

"You look beautiful," said John. "Better, even."

The weekend became a big reunion with the Andress family. Her brother and three sisters came from all over the area, and her mother even came down from her Heidi-home high up in the Alps. Everyone was so happy to see John. Naturally I was feeling out of place, but my discomfort was compounded by the fact that I couldn't stop staring at Ursula. Her face is so utterly beautiful and unique. It's as though there is an added dimension in the symmetry of her eyes, nose, and cheekbones.

What surprises anyone who gets to know Ursula is how much fun she is. "She's a clown," John told me before I met her. She's always played such icy, haughty women in films, but she's actually wild and gregarious. She uses dramatic hand gestures, is superemotional, and blushes hot-red any time she does something foolish, which is all the time. She can cry rivers without moving a muscle in her face or blinking her eyes.

I was big on my usual monosyllabic dialogue for the entire two days. Seeing John and glorious, exotic Ursula together made me scream to myself over and over again, *What is he doing with me?!* Ursula was easy with me. Not overly kind, not condescending, just natural. Many times I caught her looking at me, checking me out—that is, when I wasn't blatantly staring at her. Evidently I passed the preliminaries with Ursula, who, John told me, had given me her stamp of approval.

Just as we were entering into the final stages of postproduction, Studio Bavaria seized our film negative and locked us out of the editing room. The studio was actually very apologetic, but the investor hadn't paid the bills in months and was being charged for grand larceny in Canada. Our Judas goat of an editor had kept all of this from us, thinking he could somehow step in and gain control of the film. I thought John would kill him, but the murder was, at least, postponed when we discovered that the editor was also locked out of the editing room.

This left us with no reason to stay in Germany. But where could we go? No way could we go home. They would put John away and throw away the keys. Friends reported that John and his crimes with "the girl" were still the hot topic for gossip at dinner parties all over L.A.

We pulled out our world map to see what new place we would like to explore. Money put a damper on any thoughts of going anywhere exotic, like the Orient. We were down to about five thousand dollars. John, making an honest attempt to be responsible and do the right thing, said that he would have to go to work as soon as the money ran out.

Ironically, John was born into money as well as into "the picture business" in Hollywood, even making his world debut at Hollywood Hospital, no less, on August 12, 1926. Back then, Hollywood Boulevard was a dirt track, and the medians that still run down the center of Sunset Boulevard, Beverly Drive, and San Vicente Boulevard were later his horse-riding trails.

John's birth name was Darec Dellivan Harris, but everyone called him "Dare." As a young boy, he lived in mansions, ranches, and military boarding schools, with limousines and maids and nannies.

"Sounds like one of those ridiculously delightful films made in the thirties, right out of *My Man Godfrey*," I joked once.

"Yes, except that ours was named Chester." John replied.

When I asked him what it was like growing up in the Depression, he looked at me like I was crazy. "I don't know," he said in all seriousness. "I was unaware of it."

John's father, Lawson Harris, was quite the entrepreneur. He came west from Indiana and joined other pioneers in the early days of Hollywood. He was a producer/writer/director/actor in silent films about the Royal Canadian Mounted Police. He also produced Movie Tone-type newsreels and had a cartooning studio in competition with Walt Disney. The story goes that one day at the famous Musso & Frank Grill on Hollywood Boulevard, Lawson and his partner, Darec Ghent (whom John was named after), were drawing some new cartoon characters on the paper tablecloth and came up with Mickey Mouse and Pluto. Walt Disney was lunching at Musso's, too, and it's said that he walked off with the tablecloth after the two men left. The rest is history.

Lawson's talent wasn't limited to the entertainment business. A skilled architect, he built Los Angeles's first high-rise.

Lawson Harris was also known to be extraordinarily handsome. Norman Brokaw, chairman of the board of the William Morris talent agency, reminds me of that whenever I see him. "Lawson Harris was the most handsome, captivating man that ever came to this town," he always says.

Sadly, John's father died a slow, painful death from emphysema. His doctors suspected that his exposure to poisonous gas while fighting in France during World War I may have brought about the disease.

John's mother, Dolores Johnson, was a California native, born in San Francisco at the turn of the century. She was a great beauty and a star of silent films, famous for refusing to shoot until her violinist put her in just the right mood for the scene. Director Cecil B. DeMille told John, while they were making *The Ten Commandments*, that she was his favorite actress. Dolores starred in *The Falcon's Nest*, the film Rudolph Valentino was directing when he died suddenly from a massive infection in 1926.

The Harrises divorced soon after John was born. He couldn't remember exactly why, but said that his father was a ladies' man who went on to have many wives. John said his father told him that it was easier to serve divorce papers to a spouse than to break up with a girl-friend.

John's mother had other famous movie-star lovers and suitors. But she could never have another child because of an accident suffered while making a film. A stagecoach in which she was riding in overturned, impaling her. She married again late in her life when she fell in love with a sweet, quiet German mechanic who had a garage beneath her apartment on Santa Monica beach.

Dolores was an eccentric; mostly in the nicest sense. She claimed to have a problem "looking at anyone with dark eyes" for very long. She used to disappear for weeks at a time after taking a taxi for the 450-mile trip to San Francisco. Why? Because she liked talking to the driver. She told John that the world was his toy box and people were his toys, here for his amusement. Eventually her charmingly eccentric quirks degenerated into sad alcoholism, and she eventually died from alcohol-related problems.

All the big movie moguls of the day were frequent guests at the Harris home, including DeMille, director David O. Selznick, and Harry Cohn, the founder of Columbia Pictures. John was such a beautiful child that they were always courting the Harrises to put him in the movies. Lawson resisted until he felt that his son was old enough to make his own decisions. In 1943, at sixteen, John was signed to Selznick's famous stable of stars. Elizabeth Taylor, who was at the studio at the same time, has said that John was her first crush. She called him "Dare Handsome."

John's first film was *I'll Be Seeing You*, in which he gave fourteen-year-old Shirley Temple her first on-screen kiss. The kiss was later cut out of the film when the studio bosses decided that the public was not ready to see America's sweetheart grow up quite yet.

His second film, 1949's *Knock on Any Door* (produced by Humphrey Bogart's company, Santana Pictures Corp.), made John an overnight star. He played Nick "Pretty Boy" Romano, a young hood who kills a cop. The picture ends with Nick pulling out a comb from his back pocket and combing his hair as he is being led to the electric chair. A reporter asks, "Pretty Boy, what do you have to say?" Nick's last statement is, "Live fast, die young, and leave a good-looking corpse." Pretty Boy Romano became a cultural icon, worshiped even by the Fonz in the TV series *Happy Days*. Today people still come up to me and recite the "good-looking corpse" line.

John was under contract to Columbia, Fox, and Paramount. After some twenty films and two television series he decided that he didn't like acting and started turning down the roles that were always coming his way. John grew to hate acting probably because his father had passed along to him his own disdain of the profession. "Men build houses and women play in them," he used to say.

Now that we were all but broke, John was willing to return to film acting—albeit reluctantly. He called Urs. Over the years, she had called him many times to pass along offers of outrageous money for John to act again in a film with Alain Delon or Marcello Mastrianni or some other big European star.

"Okay, Urs, I can't go home, and I need some money," he told her. "So can you call one of those producers and tell them I'll go to work now? Put together a good deal for me."

"No, Chon, I won't do it," Ursula said firmly. "I know you. You'll say, 'Yes, yes, I'll do the film,' and at the last second you'll change your mind. You know you can't be told what to do, Chon!"

He laughed, because she was right. When he had quit acting years before, he had quit for good. Still, I think John liked knowing that the offers were there. They gave him a sense of freedom, allowing him to enjoy spending his last penny, because he knew he could always just say yes, and have an immediate income again.

Looking at the map, and our resources, we decided to go to Mexico. It was a cheap place to live, and it was close to home. Maybe John could write and sell screenplays from there. I would go home and see if I could sort out his legal problems, and I could visit him in Tijuana. The idea had a romantic and dramatic appeal to it.

According to the map, we could also visit Bermuda and the Bahamas on our way across the Atlantic Ocean; always taking advantage of every opportunity to see a new place. We spent a few days on each island and then flew to Mérida, Mexico, where we could catch another plane to Tijuana.

Mérida was a bit of a hitch. As I turned over my passport to immigration at two o'clock in the morning, the official started asking me questions. "Where is your letter from your parents?"

"What letter?" I asked.

"A minor must have a letter from the parents to enter Mexico," said the official.

John and I were taken to a tiny holding room and told that I would be sent home to California in the morning. I was demanding to be allowed to return to the Bahamas, when the chief of police, the *jefe*, with his fat belly and big mustache, came in, looked at me, then at my passport. He frowned. Then he glanced over at John, did a double take, and exclaimed, "John Derek!"

John said, "Yes." Relief all over his face.

"You and the girl, hey?" the chief said with a big grin.

John just nodded.

"No problem," said the chief, taking out a tourist visa. "Here, I just change the date of birth. Come, you must be tired. I will take you to my brother's hotel. It is very fine, and you will be my guest."

The hotel was very fine indeed. In the morning the chief came with his wife and children, and we all had lovely *huevos rancheros* for breakfast. Then the chief drove us to the airport.

It was a short trip to Tijuana, where I left John in a cute, affordable hotel and went home. Mom always made it so easy for me to come home again.

I was getting nowhere trying to learn about the specifics of con-tributing to the delinquency of a minor and statutory rape. I didn't even like saying the words. John called and said that he had just spo-ken to Linda, who was shocked to learn that he intended to live in Tijuana. He explained that he couldn't very well come home, just to be arrested.

Linda, now on the case, had her lawyer call John, and the lawyer said that, yes, John had broken all three laws. But in the real world of drugs and prostitution, a prosecutor probably wouldn't even take the case.

"So you're saying I can come home?" John asked.

"Yes," said the lawyer. "Absolutely. Wait a minute. Linda said the girl is beautiful. Is she?"

"Yes," said John.

"If I were the judge and found out that you left one beauty for another, that would piss me off," said the lawyer. "But don't worry, John, it'll never come to that."

It was swell of Linda to work everything out for John to come home. By now she was engaged to be married, and her relationship with John was settling into a comfort level almost like he had with Ursula.

For the next three months, until my eighteenth birthday, John lived in his house while I lived at my mother's. I visited him during the day but went home every single night by 10:00 P.M. This was a precaution suggested by Linda's lawyer. "No reason to get caught in the act of a felony," he said.

Some days I brought my sisters Kelly, who was thirteen, and Kerry, eleven. We would play with bullwhips and bows, shooting arrows at a target right in the living room. My sisters would hold balloons and squeal with delight when John shot them out of their hands.

We had great fun, but this new routine made me uneasy. Having my sisters around made me feel like one of the little girls. So did going home to sleep in the bed of my childhood every night. I was also troubled by the way Americans assumed that I was John's daughter; this had never happened in all the time we lived together in Europe. It was all making me very aware, for the first time, of the reality of our difference in ages. And I didn't like it.

SEVEN

If you ride a horse, sit close and tight,
If you ride a man, sit easy and light.

—BENJAMIN FRANKLIN,
POOR RICHARD'S ALMANAC, 1732

Setting up house with a teenybopper took some adjustment for John. He went from his previous wives, who were all fabulous gourmet cooks, and who, in my opinion, all spoiled him rotten. At a restaurant in Greece, I had seen Linda go into the kitchen, choose John's steak, and then cut off all the fat before he ate it. She gave him his vitamins at breakfast and carried all the money and his identification. She even told him what time it was, because he refused to wear a watch. He could put on an effective, helpless look when he wanted to. It made me want to do the mundane things for him, but I never came near the attentiveness of Linda. One day she came by the house to collect some of her cooking equipment. She said she wanted to make a soufflé. As she went rummaging through the kitchen, she opened the drawer where all the pots and pans were kept. Spiders and dust bunnies came floating out.

"Doesn't she cook?" I heard Linda ask John. I could cook. I had fed my brother and sisters many meals. But John found tuna-noodle casserole, macaroni and cheese, pork and beans, or Campbell's soup either revolting or, at best, a reminder of his days growing up in boarding schools.

I learned to make steak the way he liked it, which required only one frying pan and I kept it on the stove. John's daughter, Sean, provided relief as she moved in and out of the house as she pleased. She was a great cook, having learned from her French mother, actress Patti Behrs, and from Linda. Sean made us some beautiful meals.

John's two children were not an especially big problem for me, as children often are for most dads' girlfriends. They were both older than I: Sean by three years and John's son, Russell, by six. When I met them, I thought we would fall into an easy friendship. We belonged to the same generation. We shared similar life experiences, a common sense of history, and we liked the same music and shared many things that John and I didn't. But I found myself caught somewhere in the middle of being young and, at the same time, mature for my age. Maybe if I had shared a drink or a joint with them, we might have let our hair down and gotten close, but I preferred life sober. John was adamantly against drinking and drugs, and I didn't think it was a line I should cross with his children.

I wish now that I'd tried harder, but I didn't understand back then how important a father's love is to his children. Neither did John. Sean and Russ had been caught in the middle of an acrimonious divorce. Then they lost touch with their father completely for ten very important years when he lived in Europe with Ursula.

Linda had tried very hard to make peace between John and Sean, which brought Sean and Linda together in a beautiful friendship that will last for the rest of their lives. But there was such friction between Sean and John; their fights were so vicious. It seemed an insane way to live, and it appeared to be so destructive to Sean that I insisted that they *stop trying*. They didn't speak for seventeen years. It was my fault. Sean went on to make her own life and became a very successful writer and found her own happiness without her father. Although they made up before John died, and Sean seems to have forgiven me, I'll never know if it was the right thing to do. Those precious seventeen years of Sean's life are gone.

John and Russ had a better relationship. But Russ had become a juvenile delinquent during his father's absence, stealing cars and dealing drugs until he broke his neck in a motorcycle accident that left him a quadriplegic. Russ passed away in 2000. In the end, I loved him very much, and I miss him. Watching his courage as he dealt with his disability was nothing short of miraculous and awe-inspiring. And his insatiable will to live makes his passing all the sadder to me.

From the first day that John and I started living together, he turned over all the money to me. "It will be a good learning experience for you," he said. "Too many women are helpless, which makes them dependent on men." He left out the part that he hadn't faced the normal day-to-day paying of bills or writing checks or tipping or converting currency since he had gone off to live and work in Europe with Ursula. She spoiled him for Linda and me. Because she spoke every language of any country they found themselves in, she had taken care of all their business.

Now our combined wealth amounted to about ten thousand dollars in cash. John showed me a hidden compartment in Ursula's antique chest where we would keep it. John spent his days working on a new screenplay. I went about being a bad homemaker and continued taking care of the business as I always had. But we had never run out of money before. When our stash of cash began to dwindle, I didn't know what to do. So I handled the problem the same way I did most of my problems: I avoided it.

One day John came home and said, "The gas station asked if I had a problem with the bill. When did you pay it?"

"I'm not sure," I said.

"Well, let me see the receipt," he said.

I went to Urs's chest and pulled out a big stack of bills.

"Where are the receipts showing that you paid them?" John asked.

"I didn't pay them," I confessed. "There's no more money."

"Jesus Christ!" John said. "What do you mean there's no more money? Why didn't you tell me before?"

"I don't know."

"You can't keep putting bills in the drawer. What the hell were you thinking? That they would just go away? Shit! Now I'll have to go to work!"

I could tell by the way he spit out the word *work* that he meant he would have to go back to work at what he despised most: acting.

"Sorry," I said. "Maybe it's not such a good idea for me to take care of the money. Maybe you should do it."

"Shit, no," said John. "I don't want to deal with it either. From now on, just let me know when we are down to our last two hundred dollars. That will give me time to find work."

Thus began my education in economics. The first time I told John that it was time to go to work, he said, "The house must be worth something. See if you can get a loan."

"What kind of loan?" I asked.

"A mortgage on the house," he said.

"Oh, a mortgage," I said. A little bell went off in my head. "Like in Monopoly."

After I got a second mortgage on the house, we were soon out of money again. And again. I was dealing with loan sharks by the time I arranged for a fifth. I brought John in to the office to sign the papers. Something caught his eye, and he said, "What the fuck?! Twenty percent!"

"*Shhhh,*" I said. "It's not even legal to charge that much, and this nice man could get in a lot of trouble. It's the best I could get."

John signed the papers. Even 20 percent was better than acting to him.

Like a gift from the gods, on the same night he signed for the fifth mortgage on the house, John was offered $1 million dollars to star in a television series. That was an obscene amount of money in 1976. But the series was based on the newest, racy Harold Robbins novel, and the network just had to get John Derek to play the handsome, corrupt businessman who doesn't let anything or anybody get in his way.

Whew, that was close! I thought. *Life isn't so hard!*

I awoke in the middle of the night and noticed that John hadn't slept. I'd later learn that a night spent brooding usually led to change. Big change.

"I've been thinking," he said. "Why don't we sell the house and travel again? Let's get a van. We can drive all over the world in it, and our money would last a long time." So much for John's return to acting.

Despite our precarious financial situation, I *loved* the idea. For John, my enthusiastic reaction was one of the perks of having an eighteen-year-old lover.

I learned about escrow and sold the house really fast. By June we were driving away in our new home on wheels, off to see the world. The van wasn't an ugly old camper. Oh, no. John built the most incredible, macho-looking thing on the road. Big oversize tires, hardwood floors, an antique silver washbasin, and a contraption on the roof that opened up into a big candy-striped tent where we could sleep, leaving the downstairs for our German shepherd and Airedale terrier.

On the way, we would stop in Vegas and get married. John had always been against marriage. He hadn't even wanted to marry Linda. He knew too many men who purposely targeted married women for sex, because married women were thought to be frustrated and bored with their husbands and seeking romance with no ties. However, a woman who's just living with her man is obviously untouchable, because she's with him because she wants to be. For John, living with Linda was showing the world and especially the predatory men how much in love they were. Linda evidently didn't share his philosophy, so they married. I didn't really have a strong opinion one way or the other. What John said made sense to me, but being nineteen and having lived with him for a year and a half, I wasn't even sure that we would last through the day. I don't even remember him proposing. I think it was all part of starting a new life together and more a gesture of encouragement for me.

But the wedding itself I'll never forget. At two in the morning on June 10, 1976, we drove to Vegas, wearing jeans and sweaters. We pulled up at a little building the size of a small gas station called Wee Kirk o'the Heather. We chose it over the others on the strip because of the Scottish name. Inside there was a tiny wedding chapel decked out with plastic flowers, chipped gold paint, and imitation stonework.

There was no one about, so we knocked on a nearby door. After a while, a lady, who turned out to be the "minister," appeared. She wore pink pajamas, a bright blue chenille robe, and her hair was, honestly, in rollers. She was carrying a little pug dog under her arm. She was very happy to see us and not at all put out that we'd disturbed her rest. Without stopping to change her fuzzy slippers or put down the pug still tucked under her elbow, she led us back into the Wee Kirk chapel.

In front of us, a mother and father and their very pregnant daughter were dragging a drunken sailor to the altar for a shotgun wedding. They guided his hand to sign the marriage license. Our minister just smiled indulgently. We waited in a fake wooden pew while the semiconscious young man was hauled away with his new bride. Then it was our turn.

"We'd like a quick ceremony, please," John explained.

The minister nodded. But either she forgot or just got carried away, because she droned on and on, the little pug dog under her arm snorting loudly with every breath. The whole thing was so tacky and pathetic. At last, we stumbled out into the dawn as Mr. and Mrs. John Derek.

We spent our first night as husband and wife in our new home, parked in the parking lot of Caesars Palace. First thing the next morning, I caught a plane for St. John's, Newfoundland, the far-thest east you can go without leaving the North American conti-nent. I had gotten a job to act in a movie there. John would drive up and meet me.

The filming would be only a short detour to our travels. At least it gave us a destination. I'd considered not taking the film, but the circumstances of me getting it had been so unusual. About three months before, I had been sitting in casting agent Joyce Selznick's office with about a dozen other young actresses for what's called a general meeting. A how-do-you-do, look-at-me-for-the-future type of meeting. Joyce Selznick was a very tough, straight-to-the-point, marvelous woman. She came rushing through the waiting room with her little dachshund, trying to get past everyone without being stopped by one of the many eager actresses waiting for a moment with one of the most powerful women in Hollywood. She did a double take when she saw me, pointed, and said, "You! Come with me!"

I followed her into her office and sat in the chair she pointed to. "You must be John Derek's new girlfriend," she said, giving me a good looking-over.

She picked up the phone and said to someone on the other end, "Stay where you are! . . . No! Cancel it. I'm coming right over."

"Come with me," Joyce Selznick told me. "You're going to meet Dino."

She grabbed my hand, and led me to the window, and began to crawl out. "We'll have to sneak out," she said over her shoulder. "I'm supposed to see all those girls out there. Don't worry, it's safe. I do it all the time!" And down the fire escape we went, her dog's short little legs taking the metal stairs like a pro. We ran to our respective cars. My two big dogs were in the back of mine, an Excalibur convertible. They went berserk when they saw the little dachshund.

"Are those big monsters yours?" Joyce roared.

"Yeah, they go everywhere with me," I said. "Especially for rides in the convertible."

"I love it!"

The Excalibur was a very hot car; rated the fastest-accelerating factory-made car at the time. It was a poor-man's aluminum-and-fiberglass, chitty-chitty-bang-bang-looking copy of the 1936 Mercedes, with a Corvette engine. John had, of course, stripped the car of all its elegant appointments and covered the seats in cowhide so that it looked like some kind of jazzy Jeep. He had bought it for a road trip he had wanted to take with Linda. It would begin at the top of Alaska and end at the island of Tierra del Fuego, the southernmost tip of South America. He never made the trip, which must have been a big relief to Linda, because on a test drive to Oregon, the car didn't handle well. It was too heavy in front, which made the back end really squirrelly.

Joyce drove like a madwoman. She kept sticking her head out the window to look back at me, laughing and calling out to my dogs. The two of us parked, and she hurriedly led me into an office. I was introduced to Dino De Laurentiis, the legendary Italian producer. He was very charming, and after just a few minutes, Joyce said, "Come on, Bo, let's call John."

She got John on the phone. Although they were old friends, there were no greetings.

"John," she said, "it's Joyce Selznick. You've got to get down here right away! Dino has just gone crazy for Bo. He's going to offer her *King Kong*!"

"I'm not coming down there," John said.

"John, get down here right now," insisted Joyce. "This is the Fay Wray part! Bo is too young, and she doesn't even have an agent to look out for her. Dino wants to put her under contract."

"That's nice, but I'm not her fucking pimp!" said John. "She can take care of herself."

Joyce handed me the phone.

"Just slow down," John told me. "Listen to everything they tell you, but don't sign anything. Ask to read the script."

"I'd like to read the script," I said to Joyce.

She looked at me like I was crazy. "Look, this is the biggest break an actress can get," she said. "Every girl in this town would kill for this part. I've known John a long time. I've seen Ursula and Linda give up their careers for him. Don't let him do this to you too."

I just didn't get it. On one hand, people would warn me that John was a Svengali, a manipulator who had made Urs and Linda big stars for his own self-promoting interests. On the other, people were telling me that John would destroy my nonexistent career. All I saw was a man who was born into the business and didn't like it very much.

Joyce finally sent me home with the script and her home phone number, so that I could call her as soon as I came to my senses. She also recommended that I get a good lawyer. "You're going to need one," she said.

When I read the script, it scared me to death. It was a very difficult part, and I knew I couldn't pull it off. When I say I couldn't do it, I don't mean to infer that I felt such a responsibility to my art or that I wouldn't want to let the producers or directors down. No, I saw myself saying the words and making a complete fool of myself. The part eventually went to brilliant Jessica Lange. Thus began my reputation for turning down the most sought-after parts in town.

Dino was persistent. He began offering me anything that he was making with a girl in it. These films included *Mandingo*. The character I was to play—a little tart in the slave days of the Old South—walks up to Ken Norton, the boxer-turned-actor, and grabs his testicles while he is up on a ladder. "Sorry, Dino," I said, "I don't think this is the right part for me either."

Finally, he offered me a nice little part in a film called *Orca: The Killer Whale*, starring Richard Harris and Charlotte Rampling. Dino described it as a love story about killer whales; it was actually a *Jaws* rip-off about a killer whale with a vendetta. I thought it would be fun, and I would be able to spend some time with killer whales. I loved them and had even thought I might one day become an oceanographer—until I found out how much schooling was required. I'd play a girl who works as a deckhand until the killer whale bites off my leg, and I die. I thought it was the perfect role: absolutely nonessential. It wouldn't really matter if I was good or bad; you could cut me right out of the film, and it wouldn't make any difference to the story. It paid scale, $645 a week. Ann-Margret's lawyer helped me negotiate a contract, signing away the next seven years of my life to Dino.

I had been in St. John's for about ten days when John finally rolled into town, having driven the three thousand miles with the dogs. Damn, it was cold! Icebergs floating into the bay in June! We were together while I worked for another two weeks. Then I left to finish the film on the Mediterranean island of Malta. John put the van on a freighter to Europe, where we would meet up again.

I hadn't seen one whale yet, and when I arrived to start work in a big saltwater tank in Malta, it was clear I never would. The tank was built thirty feet above sea level, with Styrofoam icebergs and a big rubber killer whale.

I found a nice guesthouse to live in while I waited for John to arrive. It was on a pretty cove where I could snorkel almost every day. I had to work only about ten more days on the movie, but they were spread out over the next two months. Dino insisted that I stay there to watch and get experience on a set.

When a young actor showed up to play another deckhand, my eyes got me in trouble again. I don't know what it is about my eyes. I don't mean for them to send signals, and I'm not a flirt. I don't even know how to flirt. While all the other girls on the beach were learning to flirt with the boys, I was too busy surfing or sailing. The actor seemed pleasant enough. When he asked me if he could also stay in the guesthouse, I thought, *Why is he asking me? The guesthouse is not mine.* "Stay anywhere you like," I said.

At the same time, a woman named Claude called me from Monte Carlo. She was an old friend of John's and one of the original Studio 54, Andy Warhol jetsetters.

"Bo, darling, what are you doing in Malta all alone?" she asked. "You just got married! You can't be alone! I'm coming right away!"

So Claude jetted in the next day and moved in, taking the last available room in the guesthouse. We quickly became very good friends. John finally arrived and came directly to the set. I was working in a hideous scene where we pull a female killer whale up onto the boat where she aborts a fetus. (That's why her mate hunts us all the way to the arctic to kill Richard Harris.) As my husband was watching me in a little scene with the young actor, the script girl came up to John and commented, "Aren't they cute together? They make such a nice couple." She went on to tell John that the actor had confided to her that he was in love with me and I was in love with him. As I was saying my lines and waving and smiling at John, I could tell something was wrong. I knew his body language well, and his current posture told me he was furious. By the time I came off the deck of the boat, he was deep purple with rage. He said he was fed up with me giving the wrong messages and sick of what he called "little shit actors" with overactive imaginations.

A good argument could be made that John overreacted to things, and I would agree to that. He had a hair-trigger, explosive temper and felt totally justified to act any way he pleased once he had been wronged. He would get a murderous look in his eyes and would wallow around in his anger until the offender completely understood just how awful he had been. John was so articulate and convincing when he got angry that the culprit usually ended up agreeing with him. "Yes, John, you're right. I am a liar. I am a prick." Sometimes the person really meant it, but most of times I think he would just say anything to get out alive.

We were interrupted by the propman telling me that it was time for him to put my leg into a full cast for the next scene. You see, the killer whale breaks my leg before he bites it completely off. We were moving into night-shooting. Working in the dark is always exhausting. It's dangerous and strange, and I have difficulty concentrating at night. I spent the night hobbling on crutches, going back and forth from the set—where the rubber whale bit off my leg from a dozen different angles—to the sideline drama with John.

John got the young actor to come to my trailer, where he confronted him. It was horrible the way the actor stuck to his story! I couldn't believe it. He said that we had spent a lot of time together and that one night we had walked along the beach holding hands. Where was this coming from? I screamed at the actor to stop lying. Claude was absolutely hysterical. The actor said that everyone on the set knew of my feelings for him, even Richard Harris. After Claude ran to tell Richard what was happening, Richard came storming into my trailer/interrogation room. "You little fucking bastard!" he screamed at the actor. "How can you do this to Bo? She is a fine girl, and you are trying to ruin her. I love her, and I love John, you fucking little . . ."

Richard glanced over at John, and I saw them catch each other's eye. But not an outright wink. The actor ran out in tears, and John and Richard sat talking about how there is always a punk actor who thinks too much of himself and makes trouble. Richard gave me a kiss on my forehead and left to shoot the scene depicting his reaction to the whale swimming off with my leg in its mouth. John said that I had to figure out what I was doing to cause men to feel this way about me (it had happened twice before) and stop it!

Later, the actor came back with a letter of apology to me. He also said, through his tears, that John was the most amazing man that he had ever met and that he wanted to be just like him.

That was it for me. No more nice Bo. It was the birth of the Ice Queen. From then on, actors would come up to John and say, "What have I done? Why does Bo hate me?" That was just fine with me. I saw no reason to clear up any misconception. I continued the Ice Queen routine for years and must confess that I enjoyed it more than

91

I should have. I got so good at it that I could get under an actor's skin and drive him nuts. One actor got so pissed that he threw a big light stand at me, screaming, "You can't treat me this way! I'm the star of this film!"

Hah, hah. The Ice Queen routine was working.

And I used it until 1988. Until Anthony Quinn. We were making a film up in Jackson, Wyoming. The picture was in big trouble, and we all knew it, but it had to be finished. I was the producer and responsible for the mess we were in. Everything was very tense on the set. One day Tony glared at me and started taking off his clothes. "I'm quitting!" he yelled. "I've had enough! I'm fed up with you! Here's the wardrobe! I'm going home!"

I was speechless. Anthony Quinn was standing in his underwear and screaming at me. I hadn't seen this coming at all. I loved Tony!

I left the room crying. Our set was an old rustic lodge. As I ran to the back porch, my tears were freezing to my face. The Siberian blast of 1988 had come though from the Northwest, and it was forty degrees below zero. I looked around at the weird yellow streaks all over the twelve-foot snow drifts that surrounded the lodge. I had provided proper toilets, but most of the men in the crew preferred to pee and make their mark out there.

John came outside—to comfort me, I thought. Instead he said that he, too, was quitting. The picture was a disaster, and he didn't know how to fix it. I had become unbearable. I was too opinionated, he said, and the best thing I could do was to hire somebody to salvage this mess. "Fine!" I screamed. "I will!"

I stormed back to the set to explain to Tony how sorry I was and that all this really had nothing to do with him. It was about John and me. I never got a chance to say any of it. Tony grabbed me and hugged me and said, "Baby, you know I love you. But you can't talk to me the way you do. You're a girl. I've been in this business for fifty

years, and you can't talk to me that way. Don't you see, I'll do anything for Johnny! I love Johnny! I'll drop my pants for the world to
see if Johnny asks me to! But I've made seventy films, and you can't
treat me that way."

I fell apart, sobbing so hard I couldn't breathe. Iolanda, Tony's
wife, came over and took me in her arms, and I cried like a baby into
her bosom as she rocked me back and forth.

"You don't understand," she said. "You must love Tony. Tony has
to be loved, and you must adore Tony. Tony loves you, and he thinks
you hate him."

"But I don't hate Tony," I said. "I love him."

"Then you must show him," said Iolonda. "You must adore him.
Tony needs this."

When I finally caught my breath and came out of Iolanda's
breasts, Tony and John were laughing and starting to work again.

Now I'm a little more careful about the Ice Queen. I use her
when I want. But I still can't flirt.

John and I lived in the van for a year and a half, traveling all over the
U.S., Canada, and Europe. We went to the Spanish island of Ibiza to
check on a house that Ursula had built. It was falling off the cliff and
into the sea. There wasn't much we could do about it when we got
there except confirm that, "Yes, Urs, it's falling into the sea. You're
screwed."

We had no bills to pay. Once a month I would call the bank to
wire us cash wherever in the world we happened to be. Life was so
free and easy. There was no place we had to be and no time we had to
be there. Ah, but we had *huge* fights. Even with our age difference
and my nature to defer to John's opinions, living together in such
close quarters twenty-four hours a day is too much—not to mention

those blasted maps. I discovered that husbands and wives and maps make a vile combination. John drove most of the time, which made me navigator, and I'd inevitably get us lost. John would flip, then I would pout. This would sometimes go on day after day. Of course, when I was driving and *John* got us lost, he always had a good excuse. He got away with that only because I was very young.

When Europe turned bitter cold in November, we returned home to California. We parked our van in the driveway of a film producer friend and lived there for a few months. Money was running low, and by now I knew, as Ursula had said, that John would never act again, so I decided to sell the Excalibur. A friend in the car business said that we would be lucky to get five thousand dollars for it, so I put an ad in the *Los Angeles Times* for six thousand dollars. At six-thirty in the morning, the calls started coming one after the other. By ten o'clock, we had two buyers flipping a coin for the car at the asking price. By late afternoon there was another buyer with eighteen thousand dollars cash. John said, "Shit, I'd love to sell you the car. But it's sold. I got a check for six thousand dollars for it this morning."

"So send it back," said the buyer. "I will give you cash. How about twenty-five thousand dollars? I've already sold the car to a rock star for thirty-five thousand dollars. I'll paint it red and still make a nice profit."

"Sorry, but I'll give you the number of the buyer," John said.

I was dying. I knew enough about right and wrong, and sending back the man's check didn't qualify as wrong to me. I ran out to get our host, who was in the middle of a backyard barbecue. He pulled John aside and read him the riot act for being such an idiot. "Live in the real world, John!" he exclaimed. "What do you think you are, some kind of Don Quixote?"

John wouldn't budge, of course. The interesting part of the story is that Frank Rosenfelt, the future chairman of the board of MGM, was at the barbecue and witnessed the whole thing. Three years later, we would find ourselves in a big fight with David Begelman, the president of MGM, over whether Richard Harris should be in a Tarzan film we were making at the studio. I was later told that when David insinuated that John had lied about something, Frank Rosenfelt said that John Derek was the most honest man he'd ever met. David Begelman was removed from our film.

EIGHT

A horse is such a thing of beauty . . . none
will tire of looking at him.

—XENOPHON

Nothing came of *Orca* or my introduction to major motion pictures. I wasn't cut out of the film, just perfectly forgettable, and Dino never exercised his option with me. So John and I settled into our new lives as independent filmmakers.

During postproduction of our first project, I got a call from an acquaintance of John and Linda's. I had met the girl once, when I was sixteen, during my first visit to Hugh Hefner's Holmby Hills mansion. I had gone with John and Linda. That night, John had shown some pictures of me to Hef, who said, "I've never seen anything I want to defile so much." John said that I should take that as a compliment.

That was also the night I kicked Warren Beatty in the groin. I was just doing what I was told. John had said that Warren would probably be at the mansion, and that he would most likely make a pass at me. "If he does, just kick him in the nuts," John said. Sure enough, Warren was there. Sure enough, when we were introduced, he put his arms around me and, without a word, began lifting me off the ground. So I kneed him right where John had instructed. Warren just winced, grabbed his crotch, and turned away into the arms of a beautiful girl.

"Bo, I was at Hef's last night, and Blake Edwards wants to meet you for *10*," John and Linda's friend said.

"What's *10*?" I asked.

"You silly!" she said. "*10!* Everyone knows about it. There's been an international casting search for the perfect girl. A ten on the scale from one to ten. I told him about you. Vincente Minnelli was there and said, 'If she's John Derek's wife, she must be gorgeous.' Blake wants to meet you right away."

"Okay," I said and arranged to go to the studio the next day.

John, always unpredictable, jumped all over me. "You know, this will be good for you," he said. "It's time you got rejected. You should get this part. You would get this part if you were in shape and pre-pared. You shouldn't go around calling yourself an actress when you do absolutely nothing to be one. If you're going to be an actress, be a good one, be the best damn actress you can be."

I nodded, and thought, *but I am an actress! I've been paid to act—twice!* And what am I supposed to say when someone asks, "And what do *you* do, Bo?" I can hardly say, "Nothing."

John went on. "You don't study. You're fat. I'm tired of picking on you. Blake is straight. He'll tell you you're not ready."

I knew John was right. I was not too concerned about being fat; I wasn't. I wouldn't say I was at my fighting weight, but John had this peculiar way of seeing the human body. He couldn't stand fat; it offended him. He liked people lean and hard-bodied, while he preferred animals to be round and, in my opinion, fat. Our biggest fights were over the weight of our animals. I thought that if we were ever to divorce, it wouldn't be over my weight, but our pets' weight.

"It's not healthy for the dogs and the horses to be so fat," I'd say.

"They're not fat!" he'd roar. "Feel Cifi [my German shepherd and protector]. See, you can't grab anything!"

"He's lost his waist," I'd reply. "You should be able to feel his last two ribs. Animals just don't get flabby the same way people do."

Oh, he'd get so angry. And he'd purposely fatten everything on the ranch whenever I went away.

He made me a little self-conscious about my weight in the very beginning of our relationship until I realized that he had a distorted way of seeing people. This was probably why he was such a brilliant photographer. To John, everything was light and shadow, composition and proportion, lines and angles.

I went in to meet Blake and came home with the part. John grumbled, "Maybe now you'll get your act together."

I loved the script! It was hilarious, but I expected that. Blake is a genius filmmaker with a range of work that spans from *The Pink Panther* to *Days of Wine and Roses* to *Breakfast at Tiffany's*. My part was delicious; small, but integral to the story, and I could hear myself saying every single word that Blake had written. I had no fear that I would make a fool of myself. But John didn't care much for the script.

"You'll have fun in Mexico and working with Blake," he said. "But I don't think anyone's going to want to see the film."

The braids that I wore in *10* were an accident. It was just one of those chance decisions that, for unexplained reasons, lead to a fad, a fashion, and a sign of the times. I would also say that the "do" had more to do with "Bo" becoming a pop icon than anything else in the film.

Once I had the part, the pressure to live up to the perfect woman became a reality. Not for me personally—I felt far from perfect—but for Blake. It was essential to the film's humor and irony that my character, Jenny, be the ultimate male fantasy when she first comes on-screen. Dudley Moore's George Webber is so bewitched by this ethereal beauty that he stops his whole life to pursue this new bride to Mexico, where she is honeymooning. Of course, he follows her only to find that, in reality, she's not the goddess of his obsession, but a very common girl.

The most a hairdresser could do with my long, straight blonde hair was to make it big and fluffy like Farrah Fawcett's. But everybody was wearing that style in 1978. One day John said that it was too bad that I couldn't wear my hair slicked-back wet in the entire film. This was his favorite look on me. I realized that I could create that effect in the beginning of the picture with my hair pulled back under the wedding veil. But what to do for the rest of the film?

While shopping in an African-American neighborhood one day, we were admiring some of the beautiful, intricately braided patterns that so many of the women wore. It probably hit us both at the same time that this hairstyle would be perfect for *10.*

I called one of Ann-Margret's backup singers, who always wore especially tiny, fine braids, to help me. She said that she had never seen a white girl with braids, but she gave me the number of her hairdresser. The singer also told me that she wasn't sure whether my hair would braid well or support the beads. "It might all fall out," she warned me. *Oh, well, hair grows back,* I thought.

John and I went to a bead shop and chose some beautiful glass beads made in Venice. Then, we went to the hair artist's home. She lived deep in Compton, which was, at that time, the murder center of Los Angeles.

For the record: I never, *ever* intended to take credit for creating the sensation that my hairdo caused. The adage "imitation is the greatest form of flattery" sums up what I was trying to do: copy the beautiful braided styles I'd seen in the shopping mall. I never imagined that a nationwide campaign would be waged against me, including a whole hour of the Phil Donahue show devoted to singer Roberta Flack's rants about Bo Derek trying to take credit for the look that has been *theirs* for thousands of years.

This was something I knew only too well—because the artist who braided my hair said that she had braided Cleopatra's hair in a past life. All of her designs came to her in dreams, she said, and she was none too happy when John suggested that the dream she had about my hair was not flattering. Yes, John interrupted her "vision," pointing to where the braids were going straight back on my scalp above my ears (which stick out farther than he found aesthetically pleasing).

"She looks skinned," John said. "Can't you make some of the braids go forward, so they hang in front of her ears?"

"No!" snapped the woman. "I dreamed about a butterfly last night, so all braids have to go back, to look like a butterfly." She added with an angry flash of her eyes, "I only work from my dreams."

"Fuck this," said John. "I'm leaving." And he went straight out the door.

"Wait!" I said.

"Call me when you're done and I'll pick you up," he said before driving away.

I sat there for the next ten hours while the artist silently pulled and twisted my hair into hundreds of braids. I could hear gunshots and sirens accelerating with the coming of night. The artist kindly did make a few of the braids go forward, but we never discussed it.

John loved the look. So did Blake. Twenty years later, my niece just returned from a holiday in Cancún, Mexico, where her hair was braided on the beach. Melanie Griffith recently called to ask me if it was all right to go to an awards ceremony with her hair in braids, because "Antonio really likes it on me."

"It's not mine, Melanie," I said. "Enjoy it!"

* * *

Dudley Moore's part was originally to be played by George Segal. I don't know what happened, but there was a new rumor every day. George insisted that his wife get a producer's credit; George had a problem with the wardrobe, because he didn't want to show his ankles. Who knows? But the rumors as to who our new leading man would be were even better. Walter Matthau, Sean Connery, Michael Caine—I would have been content with any one of them. Finally, Blake called and said that the part had been cast.

"Dudley Moore," he said.

I drew a great big blank on the name.

"Don't worry, he's not very well known here, but he's a huge star in England," said Blake. "He's not what you would call handsome, but he has enormous appeal to women. They call him 'Cuddly Dudley.' Go see a film called *Foul Play*, and you'll see what I mean."

Well, Dudley was brilliant in *Foul Play*. But he plays a sexual pervert in that film. What was Blake thinking? John said, "Don't worry. This is just probably another one of Blake's practical jokes. When you call him, tell him you found Dudley very funny, but play it cool. He must have gotten Sean for the role."

I was sufficiently polite about Dudley when I spoke to Blake, but coolly enthusiastic. That weekend John and I were grocery shopping in the local supermarket, and I was having a bad day—except for my hair. To say that I was puffy would be an understatement; I was absurdly bloated. I can retain water like no one you've ever seen, and the braids only amplified my fat, round face with slits for eyes. As I pushed my cart around a corner, I ran smack into Dudley Moore. He had just gotten off of a plane from London and wasn't looking too good himself. He looked at me with horror and recognition. "Oh, sorry!" I gasped, then turned my cart around and took off the other way.

He must have seen my picture in Blake's office, I thought. I was running away for two reasons. First, I didn't want him to see me looking like a cow. But I also thought that it showed all over my face that I thought he couldn't possibly be my leading man. I found John where he always went first in the grocery store, straight to the ice-cream section. "It's Dudley!" I said. "He's here."

"Jesus, don't let him see you like this," said John.

"Too late. He recognized me."

A few days later, minus a few pounds of water, I officially met Dudley in Blake's office. "Good to see you again," I said. I fell under his spell immediately and found him as adorable and attractive as all the other women who have ever met him. There is just something about Dudley. I wouldn't call him cuddly; he's not round and soft. But when I'm with him, I always find myself holding his hand or leaning up against him. And it's not my nature to be touchy that way.

Filming in Mexico with Blake Edwards was just as marvelous as John had predicted. Blake takes very good care of himself and his crew. I would get to the set at about 7:00 A.M. for makeup; my hair was in braids, which required only a little Elmer's glue to keep the frizzies down.

At about 9:00 A.M., *whoop-whoop-whoop!* Blake's helicopter would deposit him on the set, and we would begin a fun day's work, surrounded by a crew comprised of some of Blake's oldest friends, some of whom he'd lived with when they were all starting out in the business and starving. Blake would wrap for the day at about four in the afternoon, because it would get awfully hot.

After three weeks in Mexico, we all came back to L.A. to finish at MGM Studios. One day Blake complained that he was having trouble with the orgy scene. It's a very funny part of the film in which

Dudley discovers through his telescope that his neighbor across the canyon is having an orgy. Dudley ends up falling down the canyon.

"What's wrong?" I asked Blake.

"I've got extras who have agreed to be nude in the scene, but they just stand around and look clumsy," said Blake. "The scene doesn't work unless Dudley sees a wild orgy through the telescope."

"You should get some porno stars," I said. "I can call some if you like."

Blake looked dumbfounded. I've always given people the impression that I'm so *nice* and sweet. I think the last thing Blake expected to come out of my mouth was an offer to round up some porno stars. I explained that John and I had just completed an adult film, and that if Blake wanted his orgy scene to look authentic, he should hire some of my friends from the porn industry.

He looked at me with a funny smirk and said, "Sure!"

Earlier that year, John and I were still living in the van, parked under a big oak tree at a friend's ranch. Our life, and our relationship, had started to stagnate. Living in a van is fine while you're moving. But when you stop in one place for too long, life can get stale. We were running out of money, and it wasn't going to be too many weeks before we were going to have the *work* discussion. We weren't getting along very well. John was beginning to believe that maybe I wouldn't find an interest. I had never promised him that I would. I was quite content following him, living his life. I found all his interests interesting. But I could tell that I was boring him.

I wanted to be like him, fascinated with everything and full of energy. But I found contemplating my navel (one of his favorite topics) futile. I slipped happily into the daily rut of sweeping out the van, cooking on the little gas stove that we had bought in Switzerland, and feeding the dogs. I can't even honestly say that I was reading any good or educational books.

Until the adult film . . .

One Sunday afternoon we went up to Hef's for dinner and a movie. Hef had one of the first theaters built in a private home, and the studios provided him with all the first run films. John and Hef had been friends since 1964, when *Playboy* published John's famous pictorial of Ursula in a waterfall.

One night, when the movie was over, we went to the kitchen for the customary hot-out-of-the-oven chocolate-chip cookies and milk. Some of the guys came in and asked the girls to come watch the next movie. The second part of a double feature at Hef's was usually the latest adult film. This was long before VCRs and video rentals, so the only way to see X-rated flicks was to go to a porno house—and they were horrible places.

Most of the girls refused to watch the next movie, saying that the films were always ugly and degrading to women, and embarrassing to watch. "All those pimples!" one girl screamed.

We were all laughing while the guys cajoled and wheedled and sweet-talked the girls in the hopes of luring them back into the theater.

Finally one girl said, "We're not going to watch anymore porn with you until John Derek makes one! John loves women and will make a beautiful film, one that we would find sexy."

"How much do you need to make one of these films, John?" the guys asked, practically in unison.

"I don't know," said John. "You sure don't need a story. And not too many actors."

The guys powwowed and told John, "We've got sixty thousand between us. Is that enough?"

"Probably," said John.

And we were off to make an adult film. Funny enough, that's when I finally sparked. It turned out that I *loved* being on the other side of the camera. John and I never sat down and decided that I would produce the film; I couldn't even have told you what a producer did. I just started helping him, taking on one task at a time, and in the end produced the film. (No, I wasn't in it. Not even a little bit.)

Making any film for sixty thousand dollars is really demanding, but making an adult film compounds any difficulty. It's like trying to work under a rock. Pornography is technically legal, but marketing and distributing it, especially across state lines, is illegal. At that point, you get into the definition of pornography, which is where everything gets very complicated. Even the Supreme Court has not been able to define pornography. So the best bet is to play it safe and keep the film's subject matter a secret.

The budget was so small that we couldn't afford to hire good technicians, so we ended up doing most of the work ourselves—music to John's ears. He loved working that way. When we were faced with a seemingly insurmountable problem, I found that if I really applied myself (something I hate to do; I swear I can feel my brain hurting from the strain) I was usually the one to come up with the solution. In the end I learned filmmaking from start to finish. I found the locations, hired crew, rented camera and lighting equipment, and took the film all the way through to the editing and post-production phase. I was nineteen years old, but not too young to produce a tiny little film.

However, our subject matter made everything more complex. Almost every deal that I negotiated invariably ended with me explaining that we were making an erotic adult movie. But I had to. "By the way, this is an erotic film that we are making. Don't worry, it's tasteful." Unfortunately, this is the same line all porno filmmakers use. I never found a way to convince people that we really were making something different. I could see in their expressions that they were thinking, *Yeah, sure, that's what they all say.* But they *all* replied, some with embarrassment, "Can we come watch?"

Making something different became a colossal endeavor. Of course, John couldn't just take the money and go shoot a pretty piece of eroticism. Nope. He had to redefine pornography! Change it forever. The project ended up taking a year and a half, at the end of which we were broke again.

The first stage of the project was research. John wanted to write a script, a rarity in the porn world. Research meant viewing all the more successful adult films in order to get a sense of what was out there and how we could make it different. As I said before, the only place to see an adult film was in a porn theater, which were vile places. They were always dark. The lights never came up before or after the movie because no one wanted to be seen or, God forbid, recognized in such a place. They smelled dank, dark, soiled, and unhealthy. The floors were sticky; everything was sticky.

But we went. I never touched anything, never used a restroom, and surely never ate the popcorn. In all the times we went to these theaters, I saw only a few other women, confirming for John the notion that he should make something different. Generally, the theater would be partly filled by men, some of whom I swear were actually wearing trench coats. I remember choosing not to think about *why* they would be wearing trench coats on a summer's day. I'm good at that.

Oh my God, porn gets boring! John finally decided we knew enough about the medium when I started falling asleep on his shoulder in the theater. "I can't take this anymore!" I insisted.

The next stage of the research was for John to talk to as many women as he could about their sexual fantasies and what they would find erotic in a film. He talked to all kinds of women: young, old, rich, poor, as many as he could. They seemed to love talking to him. It was the 1970s, and the women's movement and sexual liberation were going full-tilt. As it turned out, some of the most interesting scenes in the film came from John's conversations with some of the most conservative women.

Armed with all his research, John moved into a friend's house in Palm Springs to write the screenplay. The van, he said, was not so conducive to writing. I lived with another friend in L.A. so that I could prepare the shoot. I read many books about independent film-making and got a good sense of what John would need, and found that most everyone I came across was only too happy to teach me what I needed to know about film stock or a camera lens or a lab process.

After two weeks, John had a script called *Love You!* It was about two young couples whose sex lives are beginning to lose some zip, so they decide to swap. In our research, we had noticed a beautiful, very classy actress. She was, at the time, the biggest star of adult films, and John had written the script with her in mind for the lead. I found her living up in San Francisco, so John and I got in the van and drove up the coast to meet her in Ghirardelli Square. We sat waiting for a long time at the predetermined park bench, but she never showed. Finally, John said, "See, this is going to be a problem; these people aren't professional."

Just then, a stunning young woman came up and said, "I'm Deborah." I had noticed her sitting across from us the whole time we were waiting, but I never would have recognized her. She was dressed in an elegant dove-gray suit, heels, a Joan Crawford-style hat, and *gloves.* I felt totally frumpy in my jeans and tennis shoes. To tell the truth, this goddess of sex who must know so many sexual secrets immediately intimidated me.

John explained the project to her, and Deborah instantly jumped on board with enthusiasm at the idea of *making something different* and offered to help us with casting. She asked if we could postpone our start date, though, because she had to go home to Tennessee to testify before a grand jury. It seems that she had witnessed her "old man" get his head blown off in a drug deal that had gone bad. I remember thinking how could these words have just come out of her mouth? She looked like Loretta Young!

When Deborah returned from Tennessee, she was exhausted, and terribly thin. Behind the beautiful, sophisticated woman was a lonely, emotionally drained, and depressed little girl. We invited her to live with us; we had now moved to a little house on Balboa Island, off the coast of Newport Beach, California. The invitation wasn't made as an answer to her troubles, but perhaps she could fatten up and get healthy before we started shooting.

The rumors about John and me living with the porno queen were fantastic; I know John enjoyed them. But the reality would have been disappointing. Deborah is an amazing woman with a genius IQ. When I would take her to the local village to run errands, she would dash into the bookstore and get all excited about a new book about physics. I didn't even know what physics was. (I'm sure it was taught in one of my high-school classes, but I must have been at the beach that day.)

At night, in the little house on Balboa Island, while everyone was imagining us entangled in a wild ménage à trois, John and I would be at the dining table, budgeting and breaking down the script. Deborah would be on the couch with her new physics book, occasionally interrupting us with an especially exciting part that she thought might help me understand the concept of physics. It usually didn't, but after a few weeks of Deborah's sweet persistence and patience, the little light started to flicker in my head. I always think of my friend Deborah when I hear something about physics, but never in reference to something erotic.

I was really entering new territory with this film: an underworld of drugs, prostitution, and danger. We were making our film at the same time depicted in the 1997 movie *Boogie Nights*. I knew many of the people whose lives *Boogie Nights* was based upon (even the infamous John Holmes), but I never saw that dark side of the business. I knew it was there, though. Deborah told me all about it, and how she struggled to stay above it and keep her sense of self and dignity. John and I didn't take drugs or drink alcohol, and never partied or socialized with anyone in that industry. Our financing came from the outside, so we were never dependent on what was rumored to be a business controlled by the Mafia.

I feel we came through the whole experience better for it. We examined and dealt with some serious First Amendment issues. And we met some very interesting people who went on to become some of the most upstanding citizens in mainstream filmmaking, even children's programming.

We chose Honopu Beach on the Hawaiian island of Kauai as our location. It's one of America's most treasured and protected beaches. Accessible only by helicopter, it provided the privacy we needed. But Honopu Beach was a logistically difficult location for me to organize equipment and a campsite for all twelve of us in the cast and crew.

Every time John would get to a part of the film that would lead to a love scene, he would cut as soon as the dialogue was over and move on to something else.

"What are you doing?" I asked.

"I'll pick up the rest of the scene later," he said.

"You already have a lot of pickups to shoot!" I said. "You've got to start shooting the love scenes."

"I will," he said. "It's just not pretty when I look through the lens. And the actors are just too used to this. They're . . . brazen. These characters would be more tentative."

"Then direct them!" I said. "We need these scenes. This is what makes our film different. Otherwise we'll be making another soft-core film, like *Emmanuelle*."

I thought it funny that I was having to persuade John to shoot these scenes. He was so uncomfortable with it from the beginning. He talked to Deborah. She talked to the other actors. John played with some lighting effects to make it pretty, and we settled down to getting the film shot. He had an old lens that was once used for Marlene Dietrich's close-ups. It made pretty little stars on any highlight. This meant that I worked the spray bottle that made the pretty little stars for a special effect during a particular fantasy scene.

Making an erotic movie was never erotic. It all very quickly becomes just part of telling a story, just like any other film.

The girls up at Hef's were more than happy with the film, but there was no market for it. The porno houses didn't want to play it, and John wouldn't allow it to be shown in one. As the "old man" of one of our actresses said to John, "You made a Clairol commercial! This isn't porn. That audience wants rock and roll and sex, and you made a shampoo commercial!"

This was actually a compliment; we had accomplished what we set out to do. But it wasn't such good news for the investors, who upon seeing how much the girls liked the film, had begun to envision big dollar signs. When video became a part of everyday life, we sold the film for a nice little profit, and everyone was happy.

For *10*, I put Blake in touch with Deborah, and she arranged for the cast for the orgy scene. On the day of filming, the set was filled with a who's who of Hollywood's most powerful men and women. All of them had found some reason to come by the set to talk to Blake about one thing or another. Blake loved it. And he got his orgy scene.

NINE

Riding a horse makes gentlemen of some
and grooms of others.

—CERVANTES

I consider it a big feather in my cap to have been blacklisted by
Hollywood when I was twenty-two and in the business only for a few
years.

The buzz around town for *10* was not especially promising. I was
even hearing that the industry didn't like the film very much. Then
Blake's agent, Marty Baum, asked to represent me. I told him that I
would think about it. It wasn't that I thought I could do better; there
wasn't anybody better than Marty. But having a big, powerful agent
was a commitment to a life in Hollywood that I didn't want to think
about just yet. Finally, Marty called.

"Bo, I have never asked to represent someone three times," he
said. "This is the third time and the last time I will ask."

Put on the spot, I said yes.

Marty immediately sent me in to meet a big producer, Marty
Ransohoff. Marty was funny, frank, and had a good way with swear
words. He offered me a great part in his next film, *Change of Seasons*,
with Shirley MacLaine and Anthony Hopkins. I was thrilled. The

movie was a sophisticated comedy with an incredible cast, and I found no cringe factor in any of my dialogue as I read the script. It would begin filming in three months.

A few days later, Marty Baum called with more good news. "Bo, you're going to be on the cover of *Life*!" he said. The magazine had resumed publication after a long absence and had put the word out to all the studios that it was looking to "discover" a new ingenue. The execs at Orion Pictures, the studio that had financed *10*, had sent *Life*'s editors one of my scenes, and they chose me.

Everyone was so happy, me included. Blake and executives from Orion called to congratulate me and tell me how important this was to *10*. Marty Ransohoff called to tell me how important this was to *his* film. I remembered how important being on the cover of *Life* had been to Ann-Margret early in her career. I knew how important this was to any actress who wanted to be a movie star. I knew!

The photo editor from *Life* called and told me how important this was for me. "Yes, I know," I said. "Thank you."

He went on. "We want to re-create all the famous photos of all the great movie stars," he said. "You know, Rita Hayworth sitting on the bed in the negligee. Marilyn Monroe lying nude on the red satin."

"Gee, I don't know if that would be such a good idea," I said. "Those women were all a different type than me. They were voluptuous. I don't have their boobs or hips. I think I'll look scrawny and funny trying to look like them."

"Oh, no, it'll be great!" the editor continued. "And for the cover we want you nude, coming out of a shipping crate, or maybe a burlap sack with raffia and packing material spilling out. You know, like you've just been shipped in. Our discovery! It'll be *great!*"

"Where am I supposed to have been shipped from?" I said. "I've already been discovered a few times. But, forgetting that, it sounds a bit cheesy to me. I don't care about nudity, but I'm not really comfortable with cheesecake."

Here came the mantra again: "Don't worry, it'll be great!"

"Yes, I'm sure it'll be great," I said. "But I don't feel very good about the whole concept—copying the other girls and all."

"What would you suggest?" he finally said, ever so nicely.

"You're supposed to be discovering me," I said. "How about anything that would be . . . me?"

"Okay, sure," he said. "Tell me what would show you?"

I told him all the physical things I did that might be photogenic. Surfing, sailing, etc. "Or just pretty pictures of me would be fine," I said.

"You got it," said the editor. "Can you help us set up some surfing and sailing shots? We'll send out the photographer next week."

The photographer arrived with his beautiful model girlfriend. John and I knew his work and respected him very much. He was a very good photographer. I went to the kitchen to get Cokes for everyone. John walked into the kitchen a few minutes later. "You'd better get back out there, you've got a big problem," he said.

John stayed in the kitchen. Back in the living room, I saw the Marilyn Monroe red satin in the corner. The Rita Hayworth negligee was draped over the couch. And in the photographer's hand was a burlap sack.

"What's all this?" I asked.

"These are the 'musts,' " said the photographer.

"What's a 'must'?"

"These are the photos that I must get for the editor," he said. "Then, he said we can shoot whatever else we wanted."

I felt my ears burning. The editor had just appeased me, thinking that I would give in when the photographer arrived. I went all red with rage.

"There's been a big mistake," I said. "I'm not going to take these photos. The editor knew it, too. I'm afraid he's wasted your time."

"I don't care if we take one photo," said the photographer, shrugging. "If we don't shoot, I'll just lay by the pool at the Beverly Hills Hotel for three days and get a tan."

As usual, I couldn't think of anything clever to say. "Sounds like a fine idea," I said.

His girlfriend rolled her eyes, grabbed the costumes, and they both left.

John came in laughing.

"What's so funny?" I asked. I was shaking.

"He was a little shit," said John.

"But how did this happen? I was very clear with the editor. Didn't he listen to anything I said?"

"Oh, he listened, he didn't care, though. He knows any girl would kill to be on their magazine. Why should he take you seriously? I told you they're all shits."

Within the hour, the phone was ringing nonstop. Everyone was furious that I wouldn't take the pictures. Every single one of them seemed to think that I just needed to be stroked until my feelings weren't hurt anymore, and then I would come around. But they didn't get it. I tried as hard as I could to explain to them that I could put aside my hurt pride and do the cover, but I was never going to take a picture in a burlap bag.

The next day they tried another tactic. I was in a tiny surf shop in Marina del Rey, getting a new windsurfer for a *Playboy* photo shoot that John and I were doing. I still don't know how they found me there, but the top five executives of Orion Pictures were all on a speakerphone. They made it very clear that I was in breach of contract by refusing to do *Life* magazine.

"I know my contract pretty well, and I don't see it that way," I said, trying to sound in control.

This went back and forth for a good thirty minutes. For a bimbo, I was holding my own pretty well. When one executive would struggle to best me, another would take over and come at me from a new angle. I'm not that clever, but I was coming from a position of honesty and conviction. Finally, one executive said, "We'll sue you, Bo. This cover is worth at least a million dollars in advertising, not to mention the box office that it would generate."

"Sorry, but I don't see how this is my problem," I said.

"You know you can't beat us in court," said the executive. "With our resources, we can keep this going until you have nothing left to fight us with."

"I have nothing to fight you with now," I said.

"Then we'll win by default and take everything you have."

"Take it," I said. "You can have my rented apartment, and you can even have the old van. I'm not going to take any pictures for you now."

They'd been beating me up so long that I was getting melodramatic.

"We'll see to it that you never work again," they said.

"Ha!" I laughed. "You think that's a threat? I don't care. I'll never work for any of you again!"

"Fine, if that's the way you want it."

I tied the windsurfer to the top of the van and went home. John was pretty proud of me when I told him about the phone call. "You can kiss your career good-bye," he said. I was fine with that. I never believed I had a career to begin with; never believed I deserved one.

Marty Baum called and said that Blake had instructed him to tell me that if I didn't do the *Life* cover, I would never work for him again—including the three films for which I was already contracted. This made me sad. I would have hoped that Blake would have at least talked to me about what had happened and heard my side.

Marty Ransohoff called next. "What the fuck have you done?" he began.

"I'm sorry, Marty, I know this cover means a lot to your film, but I just couldn't do it," I said.

"I just got a call from three heavyweights at Orion and the editor of *Life* magazine telling me not to hire you, that you're trouble," Marty continued. I told him that I understood if he didn't want to hire me for *Change of Seasons* and gave him a brief version of what had happened. Finally, he said, "Fuck them." He said that he still wanted me for the film. Marty had come to Hollywood as a young, rebel producer, and I suspect that my "balls" made me more interesting to him. If it hadn't been for Marty, I might never have worked again, because Orion and *Life* made similar calls all over town. They weren't able to stop me as they had threatened, but they did their damage. I still feel it today, especially being labeled trouble.

A few weeks later, in the fall of 1979, *10* opened. John and I went to see the matinee in Westwood. The film was splendid, and I was able to enjoy all but about ten minutes of it, because that's how long I'm on-screen. I can't stand to watch myself. I get so embarrassed that I want to crawl under the seat! I never watch any of my films anymore. As we were leaving the theater, John said, "Well, that takes care of that. There goes our privacy. You're going to be a big star. The audience gasped when you came on the screen."

Although what he was saying was completely unbelievable to me, I had to wonder. John grew up in Hollywood, and when he said, "You're going to be a big star," you had to take notice.

The next morning the paparazzi had set up camp outside our apartment. Executives at Warner Bros. called to try convincing me that they had nothing to do with what Orion and *Life* had done. Warner's was only distributing the film; the execs asked if I would help promote it. At this point I didn't feel I owed anybody anything. But I wanted to keep my anger focused. I thought that by working to promote *10*, I could prove to anyone who was interested, which was no one, that it was just *those* pictures I objected to. Otherwise, I wasn't any trouble at all.

Before I could even do one newspaper or television interview, I was already being labeled a vapid bimbo being puppeted by my Svengali husband. From the media's point of view, I suppose this was a natural conclusion. There was no information on that girl in *10*. Because of my fight with the studio, I wasn't included in the film's press kit, which would normally have included a bio about me. So when some newspaper reporters found out that I was married to John Derek, they went to town on me and made me up.

My first television interviews were with Gene Shalit of the *Today* show and Merv Griffin. They were kind and professional and gentle with me, knowing that I had no experience. I still consider both of them friends today.

On the late-night TV talk show *Tomorrow*, host Tom Snyder started his interview this way: "Bo, everyone in town says you're stupid. How do you feel about that?"

I didn't know what to say. I hadn't heard that *everyone in town* thought I was stupid.

It was a difficult time for me. I wasn't savvy at interviews. Hell, I didn't even know what I thought about some of the questions I was being asked, much less know the answers. Most people—normal, everyday people, like I was—have never been asked to articulate how they feel about issues like life and death, Shakespeare, world peace, nuclear missiles, etc., etc. I didn't help change many minds with my answers, which included far too many "I don't knows." If I had even dreamed of being famous or becoming a movie star, I think I would have been more prepared for all of the traps I was falling into.

I was so discouraged and angry, and feeling as stupid as everyone seemed to think I was, when Barbara Walters called late at night. She wanted to do an interview with John and me together. John had refused all interviews up to this point. He'd quit all this years ago and had no desire to jump back in. "*I'm* not opening a fucking film," he'd say. "I don't have to do any of this shit."

I talked to Barbara for a long time and told her that I wasn't going to do any more press. But let me tell you what an odd sensation it is to have Barbara Walters call; or for Walter Cronkite to talk about you on the evening news; or that the President of the United States knows who you are. For a long time, these things always made my stomach do flip-flops, and I would blush and break out in a sweat.

I told Barbara, "Everything just gets worse every time I open my mouth, and there's no way John is going to sit down and talk to you."

"Let me talk to John," she insisted.

John took the phone. It didn't take long before I could tell that she was winning him over. I'd never seen anyone have this kind of effect on him before. He was smiling and laughing, something he rarely did anyway. Finally he hung up the phone.

"What?" I asked.

"She was charming, and I told her we would do the interview." That was all he said.

That night, John and I had a long talk. I was so unhappy and felt that this new public life was totally out of my control. John said, "You don't have to be a movie star. It's your decision. Just because everyone else wants it, doesn't mean you have to. Personally I don't think it's worth shit!"

"I think you're right," I said.

"Let's get out of town," John suggested. "The film hasn't opened anywhere else yet. It'll be a good time to think about whether you really want all this. Like being up in a balloon, you can look down on Bo and see if this is the life you want."

This idea sounded like salvation to me. I told Warner Bros. that I wouldn't be able to do any more publicity for the film, because I was skipping town.

"Where are you going?" the executives chorused.

"Not sure," I said. "John has to photograph a beautiful girl in Japan, so we'll start there. I don't start work on the Ransohoff film for another two months. Sorry."

"Would you consider doing a little publicity for us while you're in Japan?" they asked.

"How much is a little?"

"One day," they said. "Actually, if you tell us where you want to go, we'll set up one day of press in each country, and you can travel at our expense."

So began my last world tour as an anonymous person. Because of all the hoopla about Bo back home, the international press knew me, but the public didn't. One of our first stops was Australia. John hadn't been there since the war. He'd liked the Australian soldiers. "They're tough, the last ones you wanted to get in a fight with," he told me.

The press in Australia is also tough, so it wasn't the perfect place for my first press conference. The one stipulation I'd made with Warner's was that I didn't want to do any press conferences or photo shoots. I had seen press conferences on television and knew that I would fall apart under the pressure of the rapid-fire questioning. I could barely survive a one-on-one format with an obnoxious journalist. Warner's agreed that if we didn't allow photos to be taken during the trip, the magazines and newspapers would be forced to use the good material from the film.

121

When we arrived in Sydney late one night, a press conference was scheduled for the next morning. It couldn't be changed. The local Warner's representative assured me that the press would be friendly. "You're not controversial," he said. "They'll be fine."

The press conference was held at a very pretty restaurant with a lovely garden by the harbor. As I walked in with the Warner's rep (John stayed back), about a dozen photographers came running up, shoved their cameras in my face, and started taking pictures. The rep grabbed me by the elbow, and we rushed through to the back of the restaurant. Photographers can only go so fast walking backward.

We made our way to the garden, where the journalists were eating breakfast and already drinking beer out of tall glasses. The rep got to a microphone and reminded everyone that there would be no photos. The photographers sat down obediently, cameras in their laps.

One journalist apologized for the photographers' rush, and another mustached journalist asked a simple question: "Where were you born?" I could see his hand resting on my bio on the table in front of him. *Can't you read?* I wanted to say, but instead I said, sweetly, "Long Beach, California."

Another journalist asked how I liked making *10*. Another asked how did I like working with Dudley. How long did it take to do "that" to my hair? *Why* did I do "that" to my hair? It was the same old questions.

Finally, one journalist—probably getting as bored as I was—directed a question to John. "Excuse me, Mr. Derek," he said. "I've been a fan of yours since *Knock on Any Door*. Can I ask you a few questions?"

"Shoot," John said.

"Can you tell me what Harry Cohn was like?"

John gave a brief description of his relationship with the much-despised head of Columbia Pictures. "He was a real prick," John said. "We got along very well."

Everyone laughed. There were a few more questions for John about Old Hollywood, and we were all getting along famously, when the mustached one asked John, "Why do you answer all her questions for her?"

As if on cue, all the photographers started swarming again. I had no way of knowing back then what it really feels like to become a public figure, to lose some of the same constitutional rights to privacy that any other citizen enjoys. Now, after more than twenty years, lack of privacy has become a way of life for me.

The rep grabbed the microphone and yelled at them to stop. I asked them to stop. What a shock it was to my senses to find that I could ask someone to stop taking my picture and be completely ignored. I looked one man straight in the eye and said firmly, "Please *stop*." He looked right back at me with contempt and pressed the shutter button. I was incensed and reached out for his camera. My whole being wanted to smash him in the face with it. He laughed at me and pulled his camera back. *He was laughing at me!* My ears were burning again.

I turned around to John and appealed to him to do something. He said, "Fuck this, I'm leaving."

"No," I said, "you can't."

"Answer their fucking questions and let them take their fucking pictures" was his advice.

"No! I don't want to."

The cameras were getting closer and closer, in my space and in my face. So I ran. Right out of the restaurant and out into the street. I could hear shouting from the journalists and the Warner's rep calling me back. "Everything will be all right!" he kept saying. I could hear lots of "Sorry"s. As I stepped outside and hit the bright sunlight, I turned back to see about a dozen photographers tight on my tail. The limo was gone! I could hear the photographers catching up with me. "Git her!" I heard one say.

I didn't know what to do. But they weren't going to "git" me! So I took off running up the street. In the movie *A Hard Day's Night,* the Beatles always seemed to be having so much fun fleeing photographers, but here I was crying and sobbing. I turned the corner and found the limo parked under the shade of a nice, big tree, the doors locked and the driver taking a nap. I pounded on the window and screamed, "Let me in!" He did, just in the nick of time, and we drove away, ditching the photographers.

We drove around Sydney, just the two of us. He showed me the city while I wept and told him what had happened at the press conference and that my marriage was probably over. Eventually, the poor guy got my whole life story. He told me not to worry; that the Australian press isn't used to getting many celebrities. They get overexcited.

"Ever since they drove Frank Sinatra out of the country, they've been a bit rough," he said. He explained that when Frank had come for a concert the previous year, he derisively referred to female Australian journalists as prostitutes. "So they ran him out of the country, and they're pretty proud of it," he said.

It took a full two hours for me to stop crying and get up the courage to go back to the hotel and face John. I knew he would be furious that I had left him back there. He had only come along to keep me company. While getting out of the limo, I gave the driver a kiss on the cheek. "Don't worry, pretty," he said. "Everything will be all right."

As I walked through the door of our suite, I could hear people talking and laughing. I saw John and a couple of the Warner's people having what sounded like a good old time.

"Congratulations!" the rep said.

I looked at John for some clue. "I'm proud of you," he said. "You didn't take their shit."

John had just gotten back to the hotel himself, having spent the morning in a long discussion with all the journalists who were embarrassed for being such brutes. "They liked your balls," said John.

That isn't exactly what the headlines said the next day in the Australian papers. But there were big pictures of me splashed across the front page with my arm outstretched in objection of my treatment by the press. All the stories were positive, and many apologized for the press's barbaric behavior.

Down in the left-hand corner of one paper was a small photo of the Ayatollah Khomeini and a story about Americans being held hostage in Iran. The head of distribution called from Los Angeles to congratulate me for getting the film front-page coverage.

"Brilliant!" he said, as though I had orchestrated the whole thing.

From Australia we went to New Zealand, where I worked with sheepdogs. While visiting Japan, we shot beautiful photos in old Japanese bathhouses, and I dove with the pearl divers. I met my first orangutan and her tiny baby in Singapore. Slept in castles in Scotland. The trip was filled with big hotel suites, chauffeurs, and limousines everywhere we went. Everything was arranged and paid for by the studio. I'm afraid I was liking it very much and thinking that I could get used to all this, as I looked down from my lofty balloon. Not exactly the healthy perspective John had in mind for me when we left on this trip.

TEN

*The earth sings when he touches it;
the basest horn of his hoofs is more musical
than the pipes of Hermes . . . then bestride
him I soar, I am a hawk . . .*

—WILLIAM SHAKESPEARE

Back in Hollywood, hysteria was building to get Bo's Next Project. It was only made worse because we were off seeing the world. I appeared to be aloof. Our agent, Marty Baum, called us in Singapore and said that staggering offers were coming in. One group wanted me to do *Brenda Starr*. Another wanted me to do *Sheena, Queen of the Jungle*. Marvel Comics wanted to create a comic strip for me and kick it off with a big-budget film. The producer for that project was an old friend of Marty's, so Marty tipped him off that we were on our way to Paris to visit Ursula Andress.

The last time I saw Paris, we were living in the van, sleeping in fields, and peeing behind bushes. The French had been perfectly offensive and made me feel like an oaf. I remember shopping in a pharmacy. As I went down the aisle, the saleswoman would hover over me and adjust every bottle or jar that I touched. While trying on shoes, I told the saleswoman, "These shoes are too small." To which she replied: "No, Madame, your feet are too big."

This time I was the darling of Paris. John and I were living in the penthouse suite of the luxurious Plaza Athénée Hotel, with paparazzi following our every move. Ursula was in Paris to have some medical tests, because at forty-three she was going to have her first baby. She and John had a serious sit-down talk about what she was getting into and about the responsibilities of having a child.

She was very impressed with our suite and asked if we were paying for our telephone bills. We said no, and besides, we really didn't have anybody to call. She said, "Oh, *Chon*, Bo is doing so much publicity for the studio. It's worth a fortune! You should call all your friends." John said that he didn't want to abuse the situation.

"You are the cheapest stars the studio has ever seen," said Urs. "You don't drink champagne, use drugs, and call prostitutes."

You can charge all of that to the studio? I thought.

She promptly went upstairs to the bedroom and called all her friends around the world.

The producer of the Marvel Comics project was the Austrian actor Helmut Dantine. Helmut, as handsome as they come, had appeared in films such as *War and Peace* and *Mrs. Miniver.* He had recently produced *Cabaret* with Marty Baum. Helmut sent a gorgeous old Rolls-Royce limousine, right out of *Sunset Boulevard*, to collect us for dinner. The paparazzi in Paris had multiplied once they discovered that Ursula was with us. So we piled in the limo, and the chauffeur drove off through the beautiful streets of Paris. It was drizzling, which made the city even more magical than usual.

The entire time, we were followed by about a dozen cars and a few motorcycles. One very attractive photographer riding a Vespa wore four cameras around his neck. As he would come up alongside of us, a big smile on his face, he'd take his hands off the handlebars to shoot a few pictures. When the Vespa started to wobble, he would grab the handlebars to regain control.

We were taken to a spectacular apartment on the Place de la Concorde that looked like a museum, filled with gorgeous antiques and fresco ceilings. I felt so totally stupid and out of place. Our suitcases had been lost somewhere between Singapore and Paris, so I was in my travel sweats. We were served dinner by the chauffeur in his white gloves. Dinner was sweetbreads. There was no way I was going to eat sweetbreads, which upset Helmut to no end. I convinced him that I was tired and jet-lagged and that I did not want him to have something specially prepared. I waited for the dessert, which was my first chocolate soufflé—yet another element of this trip that I knew I could get used to. Helmut relaxed a bit and went on to make the presentation.

I sat on the floor, which sent Helmut into another tizzy. I explained that I've always been more comfortable on the floor. But Helmut went running through the apartment collecting all the silk brocade pillows to make me a soft place, which defeated the whole purpose of sitting on the floor. He brought out big boards bearing my image as a rock and roll crime fighter. I was stunned at the preparation that had gone into impressing me. And I *was* impressed. But it was getting very late, and I felt so exhausted that I fell asleep right there on the floor. Poor Helmut was devastated.

The next morning Marty Baum called and said that the *Brenda Starr* people would fly in to meet us in Rome; the *Sheena* people, in London. John and I went into a marathon discussion about the different projects. He didn't think that the rock and roll crime fighter was right for me. What a relief! I was looking for any reason not to do it. I was completely overwhelmed and intimidated by the enormity of the project.

Didn't they know that I wasn't an actress? Yes, I felt that I knew enough about acting to do small parts if the character was right, as in *10*. But to carry a film? To have a comic strip designed around me? I wouldn't even get a chance to learn as I go. How had I fooled all these people? I didn't *try* to fool them into thinking I was an actress. Really, I didn't. And I knew that I would have to make a decision about all of these projects soon. I hate decisions, and I was never good at articulating my reasons for turning down an offer. Naturally, these people wanted some kind of explanation. I didn't even want to meet any more nice people like Helmut Dantine, because it would mean that I would have explain how I "wasn't comfortable with the concept" or give some other phony excuse to avoid telling the truth: *I'm scared!*

"What should I do?" I asked John.

"Oh, no," he said. "I'm not touching this. This has to be your decision. I don't ever want to be the one who told you not to do this."

"Can't we just go on making our little films for now?" I asked him. "Maybe later, when I've adjusted a little better to being 'Bo,' and if the offers are still around, maybe then . . ."

"Sure," he said. "But the offers won't be around later. Count on it!"

I called Marty first thing in the morning and told him of my decision to turn down the big projects and concentrate on "little" films. I don't think he believed me; he probably was sure that I would change my mind in a few days. "What kind of little films do you want to do?" he said. "If you're in it, I can probably set it up."

"I don't know," I said. My standard answer.

John and I started to talk about different ideas for a film. He said that he remembered *Sheena, Queen of the Jungle* as a bore. "But what would be funny is Tarzan from Jane's point of view: 'Me Jane, You Tarzan,' " he said. Women's lib was all the rage at the end of 1979, and we both agreed that the idea would be funny and timely.

By the time we had finished our "See the World for the Last Time" trip, Marty Baum had made a deal for us to make *Me Jane* at MGM, with me both starring and producing. We had liked his friend Helmut Dantine so much that we asked him to be our executive producer. "Helmut is so dignified and refined, he will be good for you," said John. "I'm such a son of a bitch, I offend everybody." We moved into our offices at the sprawling MGM Studios in Culver City. What a blast to walk up to my office in the Lion Building that had been part of the old *Ben Hur* set. Me! Surfer girl! A producer? I couldn't believe it, and I never took it for granted.

It was John's suggestion that I produce. The studio didn't mind; it just wanted "Bo's next picture," and if that meant stroking the star's ego by giving her a producer's credit, fine. But that wasn't what we had in mind. John said that although my position at that moment was so powerful, it could all change overnight. "Take responsibility for your career," he'd say. "This way, you won't be able to blame anyone but yourself if you fail, or if you succeed." I planned to really produce this film. The head of production was shocked when I asked to see the weekly cost reports. And he was embarrassed when, the very first week, I discovered expenses from three other films *and* the flowers sent to welcome us to MGM all charged to our budget.

I never quite caught up with being Bo Derek, Public Figure, Sex Goddess of the Eighties, Most Beautiful Woman in the World, Good Actress, Worst Actress of the Year, Bimbo, and all the other labels that were pinned on me. It's untrue that I ever received the Worst Actress of the Decade Award—I "won" just for 1981. Nonetheless, the offers kept coming into our offices at MGM. One, from producer Richard Brooks, promised five million dollars for two films. It was the most money anybody had ever been offered at the time, and five million was a lot of money then. Obviously, I had fooled Richard Brooks, too! John liked Richard, who'd previously produced films such as *Looking for Mr. Goodbar* and *Cat on a Hot Tin Roof*. I seriously considered his offer, but I reasoned that I would be more confident carrying a film after *Me Jane*. In the meantime, Richard Brooks could develop something that wouldn't scare me to death. No such luck. I met with him, and he said that my first film absolutely had to be *Tag Team*. I was to play a female wrestler. "I'm one hundred ten pounds!" I said. "I'll look ridiculous. Can't we come up with something else?" Nope. It was *Tag Team* or no deal.

There were many offers for me to endorse some product— usually a shampoo or a cosmetic from one of the big houses like Revlon. I really didn't want to do any of them. I was having so much fun producing a Tarzan film and getting ready to play the sixteenth Jane. The millions I was being offered became as important and as real to me as Monopoly money. Turning down outrageous money is a special kind of high. A habitual one, I would come to find out later.

One day I walked into Helmut's office to talk about a production problem and found a man sitting there with an open briefcase full of cash. Helmut introduced me to the man, who was all duded up in black with silver points on his alligator boots and collar tips.

"Hello, ma'am," he drawled. "I know you've turned down all the people who want to do business with you. So we have all gotten together, and I'm here representing them. I have here a million dollars in cash and a simple three-page contract. The contract says that you will allow us to put your name on different products. You will have approval over these products—anything from sunglasses to personal-hygiene products. We already have firm offers totaling $1.5 billion in gross sales. Your take would be from five to fifteen percent."

Now, a lot of girls would go over and look at the cash, even play with it; maybe throw it up in the air. But I was speechless. I thought the whole thing was ridiculous. I said, "Thank you, I'll think about it." And I left Helmut's office.

Oh, how I'd like to have some of that money now! The fine horses I'd buy. But we don't go back, do we? Telling ourselves that we're better off is an excellent self-defense mechanism that we all carry. We're convinced that we learn important lessons from our mistakes, but I couldn't have done anything differently. I made the right decision at the time.

And at that moment, I was really more interested in solving my production problems. The big one that I was dealing with that day was with British Airways. How was I going to get our lion from Sri Lanka to the Seychelles islands, some 1,800 miles away? The chimps and orangutan fit fine in the scheduled commercial planes. But the lion cage needed a big jet. I would have to fly the lion via London, for a total of forty-eight hours in flight. For the rest of us in the commercial plane, that would be a two-and-a-half-hour flight. I felt bad making the lion go through all that, so I was in the process of chartering a 737 jet to take all of us: the crew of thirty, the equipment, four chimps, two Irish wolfhounds, the orangutan, and the lion. The twenty-foot python I'd bought in Thailand would stay in Sri Lanka. I would donate him to the zoo in Colombo. Now, why couldn't Helmut understand that these problems were much more fun than deciding whether or not I should put my name on a tampon?!

I told John how I felt about all these offers, and he was fine with my decision. "Just don't come crying later that you could have had so much money," he said, as he'd said before.

Me Jane became so much more complicated than any silly Tarzan film has a right to be. First, MGM's legal department was slowly pecking away at our screenplay to make it conform to the original 1932 film starring Johnny Weismuller and Maureen O'Sullivan. They even insisted that we reinstate the original title: *Tarzan, the Ape Man.* Looking back, we probably should have shelved the whole project. But the process took so long that by the time we started filming, we didn't realize how far we'd drifted from our initial premise.

MGM's head of production was Lew Rachmill, a studio legend who had seen it all. He wanted us to film at the Arboretum in Pasadena, California, where the original had been shot. But John wanted to shoot in the real jungle, so we spent the next two weeks scouting locations in Brazil. We eventually scrapped that idea, however, because it was too expensive and also unkind to ship trained elephants there from the U.S. Next we went to Africa and ran into the same problem. As producer, I soon realized that we would have to go where the elephants were. After all, what's a Tarzan movie without elephants?

Scouting locations for a film is the most marvelous way to travel. You have a whole list of specific sites to discover, and the local government officials want you to film in their country because a major motion picture promotes tourism like no ad campaign can. Of course, they also wanted the two million dollars that I would be bringing with me. I've been flown around in military planes, landing and taking off on dirt country roads.

We were flown around the whole of Kenya by a fabulous Frank Buck type: a young park ranger assigned to patrol huge areas of park-land with his little single-engine plane and a .45-caliber pistol in his belt, to protect himself against sophisticated poachers who would shoot at him with ground-to-air missiles. Though shipping in the elephants would be a logistical problem, Kenya was looking like a possibility, and we found some awesome, albeit impractical, remote locations.

John was a one-man show as a filmmaker. It helped that he was also a lighting cameraman and camera operator. Special shots that normally would be impossible to do because of the dozens of crew that you would have to house and transport were not a problem for us. Thanks to John, we could go in with a stripped-down crew of about eight people.

We had a formal reception with the Kenyan president out in the garden of his beautiful Victorian palace. The president was a huge man with wild eyes, dressed all in white and carrying one of those bejeweled flyswatter things in his enormous hands. He seemed to think I was pretty cute. As we all stood on a large podium, he told the assembled press that he was very excited that we were going to make a big Hollywood movie about "the Tarzan, the famous Jungle Boy" in Kenya. He went on to say that he would offer all his personal sup-port and the complete support of the Kenyan government.

Then a great big grin spread across the president's face. He introduced me as the star of the movie and announced that "Jungle Boy" would be played by a local Kenyan. That was a surprise to us! I didn't know what to say. I looked at John, who whispered that this was the producer's problem.

"Excuse me, Mr. President," I whispered. "But Tarzan was a *white* boy orphaned in the jungle and raised by apes. We have already chosen an actor from the U.S. to play Tarzan."

The president looked out at the press and laughed. He then looked down at me, bugged his eyes and said curtly that we were excused—reception over. By the time we got back to our hotel, there was a message asking us to leave the country. It went on to state that we would not be given permission to film in Kenya.

In Sri Lanka and the Seychelles islands, we found the spectacular jungles and the beautiful scenery that John needed to keep his eye stimulated and entertained. To be perfectly honest, we loved the idea of being exactly halfway around the world from Pasadena. We wanted to be as far away as we could get from MGM Studios.

Sri Lanka's elephants still toil in almost every village as beasts of burden; they're employed as the local bulldozer or for religious ceremonies. Yes, I realized that the Asian elephant is the wrong genus for Tarzan, lord of the *African* jungle. But those are some of the concessions you have to make, just as every Tarzan film has to date. As of 1981, there were no trained African elephants.

We budgeted the film for $5.5 million, a real bargain for MGM. The studio was okay about us flying off to the remote locations, even though we would not have telephone contact most of the time. John wanted to take a crew of tough, fast, nonunion workers from the independent film world, but the studio pleaded with us to take a top-notch crew. We agreed, as long as we could send them home if they couldn't keep up or if even one refused to touch a piece of equipment because *"It's not my job."* I hired thirty-five of the best and highest paid technicians in the business. Meanwhile, Lew Rachmill insisted that we be back within two months to shoot in Pasadena. He also said, "I'll bet you my life that you can't make the film for only $5.5 million."

"Don't bet your life, Lew, because I'll take your life!" John retorted, outraged.

Lew stayed cool. He said he had written down a figure on a piece of paper, then slipped it inside an envelope in the top drawer of his desk. He would reveal the number when the picture was finished.

Sri Lanka means "Splendid Isle," and it is truly a splendid place of jungles, tea plantations high in the mountains, beautiful beaches, Buddhist temples, colonial architecture left over from the days of the Raj, and kind, gentle people. Exotic, heavy smells of sweet flowers, spices, burning brush, waste, and dank humidity permeate the air. The country is, for the most part, very primitive. Wherever we went, six "snake beaters" would walk ten feet ahead of us. They carried long bamboo sticks, which they used to hit the ground in front of us to scare away the cobras. Every night, when we came home to our hotel rooms, we would shake out the bed to toss out the scorpions and vipers. Three times a day, we had to take off our boots to pull off the leeches.

The hotels we lived in were old and probably not renovated since they were built during the British colonial days of the 1800s. But they were lovely. Our room in the holy city of Kandy was made of exotic hardwoods and looked out over temple gardens. I used to watch ceremonial elephants being painted and decorated for religious rituals. At dusk I could hear the hypnotic voice of *muezzin* calling the Muslims to the mosque for prayer. We slept under mosquito nets. In a little anteroom lived Bobby, our fifty-year-old "room boy," who had worked at the hotel since he was six. He washed our clothes in the river and cooked all of our meals. He had a marvelous sense of humor and told me stories of Lord Mountbatten.

Everyone but me came down with dysentery during our three months in Sri Lanka. When the filming was over, half the crew said to me, "Thanks, Bo, I've been wanting to lose ten pounds for years!"

Food was scary and never tempting. I couldn't bear the idea of sitting down to a dinner of chicken with feathers still attached, or a juicy medium-rare steak, when every day we drove by big slabs of meat that had been hung by the roadside and painted with some sort of orange-colored potion to keep the flies off. My personal solution to the dilemma was to become a vegetarian. I developed a love for the superspicy, hot, and delicious local curries.

Feeding an average of one hundred people on the set was another problem. The locals were happy with their little packets of curry wrapped in newspapers, but the westerners were used to their traditional hot meals of meat and potatoes. After sampling the caterer's best effort to feed us with no refrigeration, I knew we were all going to die of food poisoning. So I called the crew together and said that everyone was going to have to get used to fresh fruit, hard-boiled eggs ("But don't eat them if the shell is cracked"), and Coca-Cola for the next three months. I gave everyone his own bottle opener to wear around his neck, because someone was refilling our water bottles from the nearby river.

The German camera assistant asked for hot vegetable soup.

"We're on the equator!" I said. "It's a hundred degrees!"

"Yes, but hot soup cools you," he insisted.

"If you say so," I said, thinking he was nuts.

The Cockney lighting crew wanted hot tea at four o'clock every afternoon. And the English get cranky if they don't get their tea at teatime. Many days, I happily made them tea myself and served them their biscuits. After the first week, I got into the routine of craving hot soup and tea every day.

There were many scenes where I was in the water. Many times, after John would yell, "Cut!" everyone would scream, "Run, Bo!" I'd look around and see a poisonous water snake zigzagging upstream, heading straight for me. We always had a doctor with us on the set and a cooler filled with antisnake venom. So I wasn't so concerned about snakes. But the elephant dung piles were so enormous that a person could drown in one. And the local monitor lizards were not venomous, but their bites were painful and nasty. More than once I surfaced from underwater to be looking one straight in the face. "Dive, Bo, dive!" the crew would yell.

The crew that we ended up with was absolutely wonderful, and I will always be grateful for their hard work and friendship. But in the beginning, we had a lot of duds that we sent home the first week of shooting. Some just didn't like the hard conditions. Others were just miserable SOBs who never intended to be part of a cohesive unit, something that is so essential to working in a primitive location.

Our script girl came to me after the second day of principal photography and whined, "Bo, I can't stay here another day. I am so scared of this place, I think I'm going to die here." I sent her home, then about two weeks later got a postcard from Calcutta, where she had rebooked her airplane ticket on her way home. After the first week, the makeup man came to me holding up a beautiful gold chain. "Thanks, Bo. Look what I bought with what was left over from my first week of per diem!" he said. I promptly cut everyone's per diem by half. By the end of the first week, we had sent home eighteen of the thirty-five crew members.

We had spent a fortune bringing over one of the world's foremost gorilla experts. He wore a gorilla suit and mimicked ape behavior. He was really quite an artist who had studied apes intensely and was absolutely spooky to watch.

After one day's filming where I had to come out of the water [women in wet shirts were all the rage in the early 1980s], the apeman came to me and said, "I'm so sorry, Bo, but I can't let my ape be in this film. I could see through your shirt when it was wet. I'm a born-again Christian, and I think it would be bad for my ape's reputation." So I sent him home.

Our *Tarzan* was the first Hollywood picture filmed in Sri Lanka since the Oscar-winning World War II epic *The Bridge over the River Kwai* some thirty-five years before. The *Kwai* crew had left behind all of its lighting and grip equipment, which the Sri Lankans had kept in perfect working order. It was heavy and impractical, but we used it as a way to keep costs down. Everything else I shipped in from Europe.

I came down to breakfast one morning and joined Tommy Shaw, our assistant director. "I love you, Bo," he said, "but I've just about had it with this country. I'm sick all the time, and this is all I can eat here." He was spreading jam on a piece of toast.

Trying to be funny, I said, "Tommy, do you think those are caraway seeds in your bread?! They're bugs!" I had gotten used to bugs in everything and rationalized that they were a source of protein or roughage or something good.

"Fuck this country, I'm going home," Tommy grumbled. And he did! He went to his room, packed his bags, and took the next flight home. This was a very bad development for us. Part of the reason MGM was amenable to us going off to the jungle was that we had Tommy Shaw to take care of us and look out for the studio's money. He was a superstar in the business, having served as assistant director for both Sam Peckinpah and John Huston. The only concern was whether Tommy and John, two type A personalities, could avoid killing each other. But they hit it off from the beginning. I loved Tommy's rough, no-nonsense character.

I knew that when he got home and was debriefed by the studio, MGM would call us back. We would end up in Pasadena just like Lew Rachmill had predicted. Not surprisingly, company executives were never convinced that I could handle a big production in a foreign location. And I don't think my telling them that I had learned everything about filmmaking from having produced an adult film would have persuaded them otherwise.

We continued shooting, knowing we would be cut off any day. But when Tommy went back to MGM, he told the executives not to worry about "the kids." (People still referred to John as a kid, even though he was fifty-five.) "They know what they're doing," he apparently said. "Just leave them alone." And the studio did exactly that.

ELEVEN

A horse is dangerous at both ends and
uncomfortable in the middle.

—IAN FLEMING

It's amazing the things you will do as a movie producer that you would never consider doing as an actress. Our living conditions on the *Tarzan* set were a joke. Poor Richard Harris, who played my father, had no idea what he was getting into when he negotiated a provision in his contract stipulating that his living allowance and conditions would be the same as mine. My and Richard's dressing room consisted of a young teenage boy who followed us wherever we went with a folding chair and a shade umbrella. If we had to change wardrobe, we found a bush. Hair and makeup was usually set up by my mother under a big banyan tree.

The day that Tarzan's simian buddies arrived, I went to go see them. As I walked by hugging and cooing and baby talking with the chimps, Eve and Louie, and my favorite, C. J., the orangutan, I saw a stunning lion in a cage at the end of the shelter. His eyes were locked on mine.

"Who's this?" I asked. "This isn't sweet old Rocky. I hired Rocky."

"Rocky was sick, so we brought Dandy Lion instead," said the lion man.

"Dandy Lion looks so young. How much has he worked in films?"

"Oh, this is his first," said the crew member. "But don't worry, he's a sweetheart."

All the while, Dandy wouldn't break eye contact. "I don't like the way he's looking at me," I remarked.

"Don't worry, he just likes you."

"For dinner," I joked.

In our film, the lion was Tarzan's pal, and they got along just fine. I had to work with Dandy in only one scene. In the script, Richard Harris and his bearers—the people who carry everything on safari—leave Jane at the Inland Sea so that she can take a bath while they all go to look for the entrance to the elephant's graveyard. As Jane comes out of the ocean to put on her clothes, a lion runs up the beach to get her. Jane screams and runs back to the water.

The worst thing a person can do in front of a lion is to scream and run away, which I did in take after take all day long. It brings out their predator instincts. If Dandy wanted me for dinner before, now he only had eyes for me. Tarzan somehow sees the situation. He appears out of the jungle and gestures to the lion in "lion talk" to stay back. Then Tarzan runs into the water to pull Jane to safety.

In real life, a thin but strong wire kept the lion tied to a platform buried beneath the sand. The lion man said the filament was strong enough to hold a Boeing 747. Young Dandy was usually so bored that most of the time he just sat there panting for his close-up with his eyes half-closed. The lion man had to tease him with a chicken carcass, just out of the camera frame, to get a reaction from Dandy. John was halfway down the beach, shooting with a 300 millimeter lens to get a beautiful long shot of *Tarzan* (actor Miles O'Keeffe) pulling me out of the water.

As Miles grabbed me and carried me backward up the beach toward the lion, I saw Dandy crouch real low and start twitching his tail. He was exhibiting all the threatening looks that we could never get from the lion before. Finally, Dandy snapped the wire like it was the skinny thread it appeared to be. I tried to get away.

"Let me go!" I screamed to Miles. "He's going to get me!"

Thinking I was acting, Miles just held on tighter.

"Miles, he's loose. Let me go!"

Miles stayed in character and carried me *closer* to the lion just as I saw Dandy leap off the sand, fly through the air, and pounce on top of us. I hit the sand first, with Miles on top of me and Dandy on top of us both. Dandy reared back on his hind legs and started swatting around Miles, trying to reach me with his paws. Dandy had been declawed, but most of the time lions don't use their claws to kill; claws are used to tear away the flesh *after* the kill. To kill, they use the power of their heavy paws, often breaking the necks of their prey with one sharp blow.

Miles raised himself up just enough for me to crawl out from under him and to the water, about twenty feet away. When Dandy saw that I was getting away, he sprung forward. Miles, my hero Miles, grabbed the lion by the flank and held him there—just for an instant, but that instant made all the difference. By the time the lion landed on my back, I had made it to the water's edge. But the friggin' water was going out to sea!

Dandy stood over me and started hitting me with his front paws. Each blow lifted my entire body off the sand. I felt like a mouse being swatted back and forth by our cat Coon Dog at home. The lion bent down to bite me in the shoulder—he had his fangs fully bared—but he wasn't lined up quite right and only sliced my skin. I could feel him move up on my back as his face came down alongside mine, with his mouth open, perfectly lined up to take off my shoulder.

Just then, the blessed water came rushing back, hitting Dandy in the face. He raised up sputtering and ran for dry land. I kept crawling to deeper water. When I finally turned around, I could see our art director running up to Dandy, then take off in the other direction when he realized that *he* was now the focus of Dandy's attention. The lion man ran up and socked Dandy right in the face. John, meanwhile, was running around like a madman, threatening to kill somebody. It looked like the Keystone Kops—everyone jumping up and down, hysterically.

The cool water felt so good on my bite and the big lumps that were growing all over my body. The surf was small but had perfect shape, so I started bodysurfing. A stuntman who'd wet his pants waded out into the water with me to wash his shorts. Suddenly he yelled at me to get out of the water, because he had just seen a shark! I knew all about sharks, having been scuba diving since I was a kid. *I can handle a shark*, I thought. And I stayed in the water for about another hour until Dandy was safely put away, and everything was wrapped up for the day's shooting.

The coast clear, I came out of the water, my fingers all wrinkled. The set nurse began to dress my bite, but not before the diligent chronicler John got a good picture of it. I drove (I always drove) back to the hotel with the associate producer and the art director, the three of us jammed into a pink Mini Moke, an itty-bitty Australian-made Jeep-like vehicle that looks like a "Barbie and Ken mobile." The drive back took us across a black-granite mountain pass over the island. Steering the little vehicle around the sharp turns was getting more and more difficult with my arms getting increasingly stiff and sore. Finally, I stopped to let someone else drive. The conversation in the Moke was very serious and gloomy.

"No movie is worth losing a life over," the associate producer said.

He looked over at John.

"How did this happen? If it wasn't for the wave, Bo would have been mauled."

John looked pale.

"Let's meet back at dinner," he said. "I think we've got enough material. We can probably do a quick rewrite and grab a few pick-up shots, and wrap the picture."

I went straight to the bathroom to look at the damage. As I pulled my T-shirt up over my head, I gasped. "John, come look!"

"Holy shit!" he screamed.

I was covered with lumpy black-and-blue swellings the size of grapefruits. They were all over my back, arms, and breasts. I also had a good shiner on my right eye. I took some aspirin and a nice long soak in an Epsom salts bath. Then I gingerly made my way down to the restaurant where John, the art director, and the associate producer were already deep in discussion about how to salvage the film. By the time I sat down at the table, the art director was saying, "John, I was standing next to you. You kept rolling through the whole attack. It must be an incredible piece of film."

"Yeah," the associate producer agreed. "Now, don't get mad, Bo, but couldn't we use it somehow?"

"I'm not mad," I said. "I just can't believe you're asking." I looked over at John, who had already pulled out a pencil and an art pad. He was drawing pictures and building a storyboard of the shots we already had, and drawing the ones we would need to make a complete scene out of the attack. *This is Hollywood*, I thought to myself.

The next day, all we needed was one shot of Tarzan pulling Dandy away by the ruff around his neck. John told Miles, "You don't have to do this. It's your decision. I wouldn't do it." Miles said that he didn't have any fear of Dandy. They had been buddies for three months.

As John prepared the shot (I stayed to watch from the car, not interested to look Dandy in the eye again), Miles came up to John and said that he was really sorry, but he didn't want to do the scene. "That lion has a different look in his eye," Miles said.

As the lion man was taking Dandy back to his habitat, he tripped and fell in the sand. Dandy pounced on him, and it took five men to pull him off. The lion man said that Dandy would probably never work in films again now that he'd tasted blood. Mine.

A New York film critic later said that our rubber snake looked absurd and artificial. It made me wish that I hadn't left our python in Colombo, because I would have enjoyed putting it on the critic's desk. Actually, we had tried to use a rubber snake rented from a special-effects house in Hollywood. The snake looked very realistic, and we thought we could use it for some of the long shots. In the film, Jane is standing under a tree when a python drops down and starts to strangle her. They fall into the water, when Tarzan comes to the rescue.

We got the rubber snake all wrapped around my waist and legs. "Action!" said John. I pushed off the tree, and fell down the five-foot-bank and into the water. I never even got wet; I was so buoyant from the rubber snake, like rings of inner tubes, and I looked like the Michelin man. I was so high out of the water that I couldn't even paddle my way back to shore and had to wait for someone to throw me a line and tow me back. Obviously, we needed real snakes.

When it came time to film the actual python scene, we had rented five more ten-foot pythons from the Colombo Zoo to make the scene more frightening, as though Jane had leaned up against a tree writhing with snakes. The Sri Lankan reptile man said that I would be fine. He showed me how he had taped all the pythons' mouths closed. I knew that pythons were not poisonous. But they feed so seldom that their mouths develop a nasty—and sometimes deadly—bacteria. He climbed up into the tree with his snakes (he was to drop them on me) and gave me a big, reassuring grin, wiggling his head back and forth the way the Sri Lankans do.

When the American reptile man came up to wrap our twenty-foot python around me, he was sweating and breathing hard. "You're so brave, Bo," he said nervously. "I don't know how you have the guts to do this."

"What?" I shrieked. "His mouth is taped, isn't it?"

"Yeah, look," he said, showing me his thumb, which was all bandaged up. "He bit me while I was taping his mouth. It hurts so much I can't believe it. I'm going to get a morphine shot as soon as we finish this scene."

"So how am I in danger?"

"Well, he's in a pretty bad mood today."

"Snakes have moods?" I asked.

"Yeah, and he's probably going to try to constrict."

"You mean squash me?"

"Yeah, but don't worry. We've got plenty of guys here to pull him off. But you've got to give us a sign as soon as he starts to constrict."

The reptile man started to drape the python around my waist and neck. It weighed one hundred and twenty pounds, so I had to spread my legs and brace myself to carry it. The python kept goosing me with his tail, probing for something to get it around.

I said I was ready, and the reptile man backed off. "Action!" John shouted, I started my screaming and quickly realized that the big python was not my problem. He was scared and trying to get away! So as I screamed, I held the python to my face and pretended to try pushing him away. It was the *little shits dropping down from up in the tree* that were hurting me.

For some reason, I always thought that when a snake strikes, he opens his mouth, punctures your skin with his fangs, and leaves his venom, leaving you with two puncture wounds. But when the other snakes struck, they hit my bony head with their bony heads. Hard! It sounded like somebody knocking on a door and left bruises and lumps all over my head. The Sri Lankan reptile man told me that snakes always hit hard when they strike to perform the bite and to release venom.

On the third take, the big python stopped trying to get away from me and stopped goosing me when he got a loop around my thigh with his tail. This made it much easier to act afraid of him and easier to support his weight. I was taking big gulps of air and letting out long blood-curdling screams. John yelled that it was looking great. I was acting away when suddenly I couldn't get quite enough air on the inhale. I let out a pathetic little wail and tried to get a good breath for the next one.

That's when the python started to constrict. I didn't have any air left in my lungs to tell the reptile guys I was in trouble. I never actually felt the python squeeze; he had slyly taken up a little slack each time I exhaled. Now he started to go to work on me as a python does when it breaks the ribs and pelvis of a cow so that it can swallow the animal. He closed down on everything at once. He crushed my ribs and shoulders until the reptile men heard my spine cracking like a chiropractic adjustment.

They were on the spot and unwound his coils off of me, then slapped me on the back to help me take a breath. The reptile man apologized and explained that with my long skirts, he hadn't noticed the python getting a wrap around my thigh. He assured me that as long as the python doesn't get his tail around something, he can't constrict.

Made sense to me, so we kept shooting. The next part of the scene was where I was supposed to fall into the water with the snakes. This time, the snakes and I sank like stones. I felt the mucky bottom of the lake face first, and we were one writhing, tangled mess of serpents and legs, all trying not to drown. Lucky for me, the big python freed himself first and went deeper into the lake to escape. This made it possible for me to reach the surface with the other five pythons still attached.

I came up so angry. "What the fuck were you thinking?" I said to everyone. "What made any of you think that I wouldn't drown?"

"We had men in the water to help you," said the reptile man, "but it got so murky, we couldn't find you." He added, "God, Bo, you were great!"

John was on the other side of the lake, completely oblivious to what I was angry about. Over the walkie-talkie he said, "That was great! Now let's get Tarzan in the water."

I went back in the shallower part of the lake, the writhing snakes corkscrewed around me, and waited to be rescued.

"*Ahh-ah-ah—ahy-ahhhhh!*"

I looked up and saw Miles come swinging over the lake on a vine. It was spectacular. When he reached the other side, he performed a lovely pivot; then, just as he was overhead, he let go of the vine and dropped sixty feet! Toes pointed and all. I thought for sure I was going to be speared by those pointed toes, but he landed right next to me and got on about the business of saving Jane from all the nasty serpents.

Miles showed amazing athletic prowess and courage both as Tarzan and in real life. He saved me from the lion, picked off my leeches, and kept vigil for me with the chimps; the vicious little creatures were always sneaking up to bite me. He also tapped into some secret relationship with the big tusker that all the elephant handlers, or *mahouts*, admired.

But on a purely superficial note, Miles had the most beautiful body I have ever seen. It all started with his divine, beautifully aligned bone structure. A horse breeder develops a fairly proficient eye for what's called confirmation. First we discern the skeleton, the most essential element to the athleticism and pure beauty of a horse. It's the framework upon which everything else is built. An untrained eye will see only the coloring and showy parts of a horse. We call them "mane-and-tail buyers." They look at horses the way some men look at women, noticing only big hair and big boobs.

My Spanish and Portuguese horses are judged strictly on their confirmation to even be entered in the *studbook*, an official record of a purebred's pedigree. And guess what? It's based on a point system on a scale of one to ten. Everything about the horse is taken into consideration: condition, coloring, markings, temperament, even the little sworls or cowlicks. But most important are the degrees of angles and lines of the skeleton, which will have a direct influence on the final category: movement. Miles would have scored well in a studbook. I should have been nicer to Miles. He was a true southern gentleman, a really terrific guy, but the Ice Queen was in full power then.

Our film was the quick and dirty Tarzan compared to the big-budget Warner Bros. movie *The Legend of Greystoke: Tarzan, Lord of the Apes*. It had been in preproduction for over a year when we came along. Edgar Rice Burroughs had only once made the mistake of selling the rights to one of his books in perpetuity—to MGM in 1931. This is how we were able to make our film and why we had to constantly alter it to conform to the original MGM classic. For example, the leader of the bearers had to fall off the African escarpment. A bearer had to be eaten by a lion in the night. On and on, the legal department would pick away at us.

When Warner Bros. paid a fortune to the Burroughs estate for the rights to *Tarzan*, the studio was evidently under the impression that it was paying for the rights to *all Tarzan* movies and that no other *Tarzan* would be made at the same time as *Greystoke*. So when our film was announced, all hell broke loose, and Warner Bros. sued the Burroughs estate for fraud.

The editing phase of our film was a mad rush. A three-month actors' strike in 1980 had left the studios with no new pictures for summer 1981, causing a near financial disaster for the whole industry. Normally the postproduction phase of a film takes six months to a year. Although we had completed principal photography in the first week of April, MGM asked if we could have the film ready for a June 28 release. *Tarzan* certainly was not a big film that required a whole year, but to think that postproduction could be completed in anything less than three months was insane. The studio execs pleaded with John, promising to give us anything we needed. The whole studio would be at our disposal. We could hire more technicians, pay overtime, have priority at the lab, whatever we wanted.

"Can I take the film off the lot?" I asked Frank Rosenfelt, chairman of MGM.

"Why?" he replied. "MGM has the best facilities in town."

"I don't like your sound department," I said. "They're old-fashioned, slow, and have a very lax attitude. I want to take the picture to an independent studio, where the technicians are the best and they're fast."

The chairman was dumbfounded at the thought that he didn't have the best of everything at the studio. "Sure, Bo, whatever you say," he said. Then Frank promptly ordered a complete overhaul of the MGM postproduction department.

During editing, MGM was sued by the Burroughs estate. The estate's attorneys were trying to stop the release of our film, claiming that it wasn't a true remake and that we had made too many changes to the original. Mind you, they hadn't actually *seen* our film. No one had; it wasn't finished yet. But if the lawyers could tie MGM up in court and delay the movie's release, they would be covering their behinds in their lawsuit with Warner Bros.

The estate made many absurd claims and accusations, one being that we had made Tarzan "too sexy." But MGM's remake clause said something to the effect that we could bring the story up to the standards and mores of the time. There wasn't even a love scene in our film, just some seminudity, and in 1981 almost every film had nudity. So the legal department determined that we were in the clear there. But the press had a field day with it, saying that those filthy Dereks were ruining the reputation of Tarzan. The owner of an orangutan that was not even in our film sued us for twenty million dollars, claiming defamation of his animal's image.

All this over a silly Tarzan movie!

The case was heard in a New York federal court while we were still scoring the movie. The judge ordered that a print of the unfinished film be brought to court so that he could determine whether or not we had conformed sufficiently to the original. At this point, we were not overly concerned, although no filmmaker wants his or her film seen before it's finished.

Our assistant editor and an MGM executive took the print to New York. Very late one night, the studio called to inform us that the judge had viewed the film; now all we could do was to wait for his decision. Even later that night, we got a call from the assistant editor saying that the judge had watched the film *again* on an editing machine. This time he'd actually taken a grease pencil to the print, marking where the film should be cut. In the editor's opinion, the judge's cuts had nothing to do with story content or with making the film conform to the original. He said that he was returning to California with the print and would meet us in the editing room first thing in the morning.

John put on two sets of glasses, looked me over, and said,
"Good, your face is clean, let's go to work."

The Collins kids, an independent, well-working little unit.

Me, my mother, Kelly, my father, and Colin, Christmas 1962.
What a bunch of goofballs.

Typical California girl at fifteen.

Every weekend we had to sail; it was part of Dad's job!

Windsurfing on Lake Powell, Utah, our favorite camping spot, 1979.

Mykonos, 1973, with my friend Yanoula.

The Excalibur, my dogs' favorite car.

I almost played Eve in my favorite project that never got made.

Another photo from the first time John photographed me. Linda held the lights.

Sweet Dudley. We went through such a life-changing experience together.

The controversial cornrows.

You'd never know John just screamed to Kerry, "Just take the fucking picture!"

The crazy things you'll do when you're the director.

Mouro, my favorite stallion, all zest and gusto.

Bullfighting at the Peralta Ranch in Seville, Spain.

The leather bikini John made for me.

I've always been a cowgirl.

John called this photo "Attitude."

Shopping with Ursula in Paris always makes the paparazzi go wild.

John's leather shop, where he made me such beautiful things.

Foals have the sweetest breath.

I was a midwife at her birth.

Sri Lanka, 1988. She fell asleep with her trunk in her mouth.

Singapore, 1980. You should have seen his face when I suggested he stop smoking.

Riding with Kerry.

Playing cards between races. Jockeys are my absolute heroes.

A horse-crazy girl's dream come true.

Predictably, John went crazy and woke up every studio executive he knew. In my twenty-five years of knowing John, I don't remember him ever hesitating to call someone in the middle of the night. He had such a sense of conviction that he never had the same doubts and insecurities as most of us. The executives already knew what had happened with the judge, but they'd hoped to keep it from us as long as possible.

In the morning, we looked at the film with about a dozen of our editing crew and the legal department. All of us realized that the marks that the judge had made cut out only bits and pieces of nudity. According to the lawsuit, the judge could determine whether or not nudity was part of bringing our remake up to current-day standards and mores. But that should mean either nudity or no nudity, not arbitrarily cutting out half a nude shot here and half there. Not to mention all the jump cuts the judge's edits would cause. For instance, in one scene I was reaching for a chimp. The judge wanted twenty frames cut, meaning that the movement of my arm would jump from resting at my side to touching the chimp's face.

John took off running to the Thalberg Building, where all the MGM executives had their offices. I followed. As we ran past the guard at the gate, he said, "Good morning, John."

"This morning is fucked, Bill!" said John.

"Go get 'em, John," Bill said.

Then I came running past. "Good morning, Bo," said Bill.

"Morning, Bill."

"Go get 'em, Bo!"

"Oh, we'll try."

Bill was accustomed to seeing us run by his gate on our way to confrontations with the executives. Bill was great; he had been at that same gate in the days when John was an actor. And he used to let me sneak my dogs onto the lot.

By the time I came huffing and puffing into the chairman's office, John was screaming about the First Amendment. John was amazing when he got angry. His usual scattered memory became flawless, and his tongue sharpened. Sometimes he made up a word, but anyone would agree that it was the *perfect* word.

The executives were all trying to calm down my husband. "John, please understand that if you just make these cuts, the judge will let us release the film," they said. "You have to agree that the cuts don't really change the integrity of the film."

"Push back the release of the film," John insisted. "You've got to fight this."

"But, John, yours is the only film we have for the summer!"

"Look, if the judge was ordering cuts to make the film conform to the old one, I'd be fine with that," John said. "But this is about censorship. A fucking federal judge has just tried to censor a film!"

He turned to an executive from the legal department. "Has this ever happened before in the United States?"

"Never," the man said. "I agree with you; this is a huge First Amendment issue."

Another executive piped up, "John, if this was any other time, if there hadn't been an actors' strike, if we had another film ready for release—I promise you we would fight this to the end. But we just can't do it this time."

There was nothing we could do except present our case to the media, which we did, sure that the press would be as outraged as we were. But they were more interested in twisting the story and reporting that some lewd scenes had to be cut from *Tarzan*. John went a bit wild a couple of times and once was quoted on the front page of the trade papers as saying, "Blood will flow on the streets of Culver City if the film is cut!"

Ironically, the only journalist to accurately follow the story was entertainment reporter Rona Barrett, who would call us daily and report the truth on *Good Morning America*.

I brought the film in on schedule and under budget. It opened to mostly scathing reviews but did very well at the box office, breaking all records for the first week. The press never stood up for us. But, of course, the controversy was over a silly Tarzan movie. I thoroughly believe that if the film's subject matter had been more substantial, we would have had national support at the idea of government censorship. I am still so disappointed.

TWELVE

The outside of a horse is good for
the inside of a man.

—WINSTON CHURCHILL

While working on *Tarzan*, we had moved into a hotel in Marina del
Rey, which was a convenient fifteen-minute drive to MGM. I was
feeling restless; maybe my biological clock was ticking. With offers
of huge money coming in, I was beginning to feel worthy of a little
house of my own. In my sixteen years with John, we had lived in
hotels or the van, except for the year we had lived in his house in L.A.
I say "John's house" because he paid for it, but in reality it was always
Ursula's. Although John and Linda had lived there for ten years
when I moved in, I never had the sensation of moving into "Linda's
house." Ursula just has a way about her: whatever and whomever she
touches is always hers—John included. You would think that Linda
and I would have felt threatened or jealous, but Urs touched Linda,
and she touched me too. So we are hers as well.

John had grown up on various ranches and ranchettes around
Los Angeles and had always hoped to live with horses again, but his
wives would never move out of town. To them, the San Fernando
Valley qualified as "the country." I had wanted a ranch for as long as

159

I could remember; it fell right in line with my childhood stallion dream, but John was dead set against it. He thought I would get bored. After all, I had never lived in the country before. "Girls get lonely and don't like the solitude," he said.

We looked at pretty houses around L.A. But I knew exactly where I wanted to live: Santa Ynez Valley. Any time that we were traveling north in the van, we would stop there for the night and camp in the public parking lot. I remember saying each time, "Wouldn't this be a nice place to live and have horses?"

One weekend, at my insistence, we drove the two and a half hours from L.A. to Santa Ynez, walked into a real-estate office, and told the agent that we wanted a little California ranch house. A fixer-upper would do. Something modest but with character. The agent took us to a few houses that fit the bill, save for the character part. Then the agent said, "There is a house you should see. It's not what you are looking for at all, but it's such an unusual house."

As we drove up the pepper-tree-lined driveway, I looked at John, he looked at me, and we both knew that we would live in this house. It sat atop a hill with a spectacular 360-degree view of rolling hills and oak trees, framed by the Los Padres National Forest and the Santa Barbara Mountains.

The house was a classic Spanish style, very similar to the *fincas* we'd seen in Ibiza when we went to inspect Ursula's house—the one that was falling into the sea. On one side sat a lovely stable. The agent was right: it wasn't at all what we were looking for. But we *had* to have it.

I wrote a check for fifty thousand dollars as a down payment—every penny we had—and just like that we became the proud new owners of a beautiful five-thousand-square-foot house on forty-six acres. We'd figure out how to pay for it later.

I immediately took to ranch life. I loved the isolation and the blessed solitude, free of the persistent hiss of traffic and the din of city life. I was to live on the ranch for twenty years, but I don't think I ever felt that the ranch was *mine*, that I really owned it. I'd never had the opportunity to associate so much beauty and fun with a place where I lived. I'd always had to *go* to a place as wonderful as the ranch. I always had the feeling that I was on vacation, especially in the mornings. I couldn't believe that life had somehow placed me in that special spot on that wonderful piece of the planet. I suppose every landowner gets that same sense of awe at the idea that you can walk up to a globe of the earth and spin it until you find that pinhead-sized place that is *yours*.

I loved waking up early and having chores; it had been a long time since I'd had any. I had become a virtual magician at packing a suitcase, but the normal day-to-day pattern of living was new to me. I adored it. I love manual labor. My favorite days were the ones that began with a problem; perhaps a broken water line or fence rail. Anything that gave me the opportunity to run down to the tool shed was fine with me. I kept an impeccably organized shed, collecting all the tools in my belt so that I'd always be ready to repair things. Fixing things gives me a great sense of self-worth and satisfaction.

Laboring in the heat of the day has always appealed to me—a good thing, because I hate gymnasiums. I would rather dig a ditch to trim my torso or hammer nails to strengthen my arms any day than go to a gym. And I'm not so sure it's good for my mental health to exercise mindlessly on a static machine while watching myself in the mirror for the hour it would take to work out. Over the years, I've tried it all: every new machine, the best system, the latest method, personal trainers, group classes, this diet and that food-combination approach to eating. All they ever did was make me obsess about what I put in my mouth and how many tricep arm-raises I had done in a day.

I remember coming home to the ranch after shooting *Bolero* and resolving to just relax and not worry about my shape for a while.

Postproduction on the film would take a good six months to complete *Oh boy*, I thought to myself. *I'd eat whatever I want and not do a single leg squat. I'm just going to enjoy myself. Maybe even get fat!*

But the ranch kept me busy.

From that day on, I've never had to worry about my weight. Yes, if I haven't been doing enough manual labor, I do a few basic, old-fashioned calisthenics-type exercise; push-ups, sit-ups, but no more exotic stuff. I can get just as good a workout cleaning my house as I can spending an hour on any trick or high-tech machines. I dread the moment that dinner conversation turns to diet or exercise—and in L.A., it will. It's such a bore! I say get on with it. Get fat. Wear a muumuu. But stop worrying about it, and be happy!

John taught me to ride horses. He was an expert horseman and a fanatic about safety. He would eat you up and spit you out if you did something reckless or stupid around a horse. If he could bring you to tears about how close you had come to killing yourself, even better.

I had been on horse rides before, but there is a gigantic difference between riding and simply staying on. John taught me about *light hands*. The first thing he did was to take a bridle with a simple grazing bit (considered to be extremely kind to the horse) and rig it up to hang from my upturned elbow so that the bit fit around my wrist. Then he pulled on the reins.

"Ouch!" I shrieked. The leverage of the shank on the bit was crushing my wrist.

"There, now you know what you are doing to the horse's mouth every time you pull too hard on the reins," said John.

I got the message.

"You can use the bit as a form of communication between you and the horse, or as an instrument of torture," he said. "It's all in your hands."

John taught me to have a *good seat*. I had pretty decent balance from surfing and motorcycle riding, but he showed me how a horse will respond to the slightest shift of weight or tilt of your body in the saddle.

He laid the groundwork within my body so that I'm able to ride, with a fair amount of finesse, just about any horse I want. Still, there are many horses I won't ride. It's a good thing to listen to your instincts and follow your intuition around horses. Some just have a bad look in their eyes or a sourness that shows all over their body.

My first horse was a lovely, entertaining Arabian gelding named Star: a bright chestnut with four white socks and a big star on his forehead. I renamed him Houdini after only one month because he was such an amazing escape artist, always getting out of wherever we put him.

John would yell at me, "You forgot to latch the gate!"

"I did latch it!" I'd insist.

One day John and I returned from lunch at the local Longhorn Cafe. I opened the heavy barn door to find all the horses out of their stalls and eating from the feed. It's very dangerous for a horse to eat too much rich food; it's actually toxic to their system.

"I swear I latched all the stall doors," I said to John as we shooed the horses back into their stalls. "Wait a minute; where's Star?"

We found him in a stall, looking like the very picture of innocence. But it wasn't his stall. He had used his mouth to undo the latch on his stall—an extraordinary feat—and proceeded to let out all the other horses. Then he put himself in the wrong stall *and* closed the door. The only thing he couldn't manage to do was to relatch the door, but I was vindicated. Star had a new name, and I had to install magician-proof latches on the stall doors.

Another time, I found Houdini in a holding pen, fiddling with the latch on the gate.

"Houdini, don't you dare!" I called out to him.

He undid the latch, swung open the gate with his muzzle, and turned to give me a look that could translate only to "Fuck you!" Then he ran off down the hill, bucking and farting.

John went through a strange transformation at the ranch: He stopped riding horses. John Derek, the most opinionated expert on the subject of training animals. My John, who'd studied dogs with Larry Trimble (legendary trainer of Strongheart, the first German shepherd to star in motion pictures) and Carl Spitz (founder of the U.S. Army's War Dogs program during World War II) and horses with Ralph McCutcheon (trainer of the Lone Ranger's Silver, the Cisco Kid's Diablo, and so many other movie-star horses). He just stopped riding.

I'd had this romantic notion that we would gallop off into sunsets together. But except for the times when I got stuck on some riding technique, like a lead change—and John would handily mount and beautifully demonstrate what he was trying to teach me—he wouldn't ride. I finally confronted him after he'd made up some lame excuse about why he couldn't go on a trail ride with me. "*I* don't want to walk up all those fucking steep hills," he grumbled. "Why should I make a horse take me up them on his back?"

"But didn't we buy the ranch to enjoy horses together?" I asked.

"I'm enjoying them," he said. "I love watching you."

"By myself," I said.

"*I* can't stand being told what to do, and I don't want to tell an animal what to do anymore," he said.

"So am *I* supposed to start feeling guilty about inflicting my will on them?"

"No. It's just some hang-up I have now."

John's new hang-up threw me for a loop—for about a minute. He continued to be my equine educator, and he remained as obstinate and opinionated about what I might be doing wrong as ever before. As for me, I had a *ranch!* With horses and dogs and cats and deer and wild boar and bobcats and puma and owls and vultures to play with.

John set up a leather shop. It was very rustic and macho, with walls of rough-sawn cedar and antique sewing machines, including one big, black behemoth powerful enough to sew through a good half an inch of harness leather. John was very talented with his hands. He was a perfectionist by nature, especially all things visual and tactile. The first thing he would do when examining a beautiful table made of an exotic hardwood was to admire the visual beauty of the style and line and proportions. Then it had to pass the "touch" test. He would run his hands over the top (and it had better feel like warm glass), continuing across all the corners and grooves and the underside of the table.

"Why do you care about what's underneath?" I would ask.

"If you can't reach under and enjoy the feel of it while you're eating or having interesting conversation, what good is it?" he'd say.

John spent a lot of time in his shop making things for me, Linda, and Ursula (the wives), and for very close friends. But only those friends who would truly appreciate the suffering that went into making a perfect "something." Watching him, you'd never know he enjoyed his time in the shop. I'd usually find him bitching and cursing a piece that was giving him trouble, one that was not living up to his standards. Leather is very difficult to work with. I know, because my grandmother taught me to sew. Whereas fabric lays there flat and malleable, each leather hide has its own peculiar grain and thick spots, all of which must be coaxed and tugged into shape. Every one of John's creations was inscribed with a personal note. Into a particularly uncooperative, but lusciously soft and buttery, tobacco-colored deerskin vest that he made for our friend Layla, he wrote:

1 of 1. And when this "one" returns to the pits of hell from whence it came . . . it, like the Dodo bird, will be Extinct.

APRIL–MAY '94

He made me leather boots, chaps, saddles, shirts, and miniskirts. He even made me the leather bikini that I wore in my first *Playboy* layout. Many retail leather businesses copied the bikini and put my picture on their walls and claimed to have made it. But it was John's.

Regarding my *Playboy* shoot, I suppose I should explain my attitude toward nudity, because it's considered so offensive in America. I find this so hypocritical. Why is it all right to be base and outright vulgar as long as you have three little patches of your body covered with thin pieces of fabric? But, Oh Mercy Me, don't take off your clothes! And what about the way people glamorize and accept hideous violence in movies as a form of entertainment? As Jack Nicholson once said, "If you hack off a woman's breast with a meat ax, it's a PG. But if you kiss it, it's an NC-17." Why is it okay for a singer to get up onstage and bump and grind her hips, shamelessly seducing the audience? As long as a little cross rests in her cleavage and she thanks Jesus when she receives an award, "She's a good girl," they'll all say.

I'm not an exhibitionist. I don't go out in sexy or revealing dresses, and these days I wouldn't get caught dead in a bikini at the beach. It causes too much trouble, and people stare because of who I am. Those days are over.

I've been on the cover of *Playboy* a record five times. It was never about me presenting myself in the magazine. It was about John's photography. He photographed all the layouts, and I think they are beautiful. No dripping-wet lips. No bedroom eyes. No coarse or vulgar poses. Just beautiful photos of a subject *without clothes*. Just as artists have been painting or sculpting or photographing the human form forever.

Every time John got ready to send in the photos to *Playboy*, he would say, "They're not going to like them. There are no crotch shots." But *Playboy* always ran them, and my issues made record sales.

I don't know where I got my opinion on nudity. I wasn't brought up by hippie-type parents who told me that my body was a temple, although I was probably influenced by the Akira Kurosawa samurai films that my father used to take us to see at the drive-in. They usually contained nudity. I remember finding the bodies beautiful, but then, the characters were never being vulgar while without clothes. I guess I have a more European attitude toward nakedness. Growing up on the beach, I never found much difference between being nude and some of the itty-bitty bikinis we all wore.

THIRTEEN

I have seen the Spanish horse receive
knife wounds on the face and remain firm
as if he were made of Bronze.

—LUIS DE BANUELOS

The movie *Bolero* was born as a result of a bad night of shadowy gloom—not a favorable climate for conceiving a movie. John was in one of *those* moods; one of those up-all-night brooding moods that usually sent us off on another adventure. Earlier in the day, we had walked away from a dream deal with Universal Studios to make a film titled *Eve and That Damned Apple*, a comedy based on Mark Twain's *The Diaries of Adam and Eve*. I loved this project, and the script was actually very good—not something John usually made a priority. I've always believed in the old Hollywood expression "It's got to be there on the page." But John, well, he was far too artistic and a bit too abstract to be tied to such rules.

Everything was all set to go on the film. We had been to New Zealand and found magical locations for the Garden of Eden scenes. Universal was giving us a luxurious $7.5 million to make the film, $2 million more than we had for *Tarzan*. We were in the midst of casting, and for the first time I really sensed that we had everything going for us. It felt like we were going to make a genuine, honest-to-God movie with a beginning, middle, and end.

But, as they say, the gods got jealous and threw a wrench in our wheel, namely a senior executive of the studio. He concocted this absurd fantasy that I was scheming against him, that I had arranged for the writer of our screenplay to write another *Eve and That Damned Apple*, and that I was hiding this latest version from him.

I didn't know what was causing him to behave this way. All I knew was that he had abruptly stopped taking my calls and had ordered every copy of our script gathered from every department in the studio (meaning dozens and dozens of copies). Then he ordered his staff to read each copy, compare it with all the others, with instructions to find the version of the script that he was convinced I was hiding from him. In the midst of all the hysteria, he accused me of lying to him. That was it for me and, of course, for John. *Film over.*

Lew Wasserman, the chairman of Universal, called us that same morning to convince us to come back. He said that *Eve and That Damned Apple* had been the easiest project to sell to distributors in years. If we came back, he promised that we would never have to deal with the paranoid executive ever again. We had just come from the same kind of screwy situation at MGM, where the president, David Begelman, had been removed from our film. It's a lousy way to make a movie. So we declined the offer.

The rest of the day was very odd. I fed the animals and scooped up their shit from all over our property. I watered the garden, killed as many snails as I could find, and went about the normal routine of a day at the ranch. I'd catch myself sighing, relieved that the sick drama was over. At the same time, I was a bit anxious. We had just burned another bridge. A big one.

That night in bed, John and I reviewed our options for the future.

"Maybe we shouldn't be so high and mighty in a business full of pricks," John said.

"Maybe we should just take the money and run," I said.

Finally, John started laughing. "Fuck it!" he said. "Every project that you're offered is just another version of the scene from *10*. They just want to see you fuck to 'Bolero' again. Let's go make a film called *Bolero.*"

We had a good chuckle and went back to our options, which seriously included giving it all up again. We could return to independent filmmaking, but we would clearly have to leave me out of the films. It had been folly to think that any film that included me would be considered little or independent, no matter how small the budget. *Bo* was too much a curiosity to the public and too much fun for the press.

My problem with giving it all up was that I was blissfully happy with my new life on the ranch, even the picking-up-the-shit part. Not to mention my growing passion for everything horses. The underground world of art films was fun, but it would never pay for my new horse habit.

I had just received a gift of a beautiful book titled *All Those Girls in Love with Horses*, by author-photographer Robert Vavra. The book portrays eleven young horsewomen from around the world. Among them is a gorgeous Spanish girl, with raven-black hair down to her waist, riding white stallions at the Royal Andalusian Riding School in Jerez de la Frontera, Spain. In a rare moment of inspiration, I reminded John about the girl in Vavra's book and said, "Let's go make something beautiful and romantic in Spain." All the while, I was thinking, *I could ride horses like that girl in the book.*

The next morning I called our agent, Marty Baum, to see what he thought about the idea. He said, "If you really want to make a motion picture and be left alone, there are two new guys in town from Israel, Yoram Globus and Menahem Golan."

Marty put the deal together in a day. No script, no cast, not even a story, but Golan and Globus's Cannon Films agreed to give us five million dollars to make a horse movie called *Bolero* because *Bo is into horses.* Crazy way to make movies, but *Tarzan* had been a financial success, and Yoram and Menahem wanted my next film. The two Israeli cousins seemed nice enough, and the contract, which was a total of five pages (in contrast to the typically voluminous Hollywood contract), said exactly what Marty promised: they'd put up the money and leave us alone.

A few days later, John and I took off to Spain to get inspired. Our plan was to find locations that caught his fancy and then work with a writer on the script when we returned home. John liked working that way. Yes, it was putting the horse before the cart, but that was John.

We arrived in Seville in the afternoon, feeling cruddy from jet lag. I didn't notice anything but the back of the taxi driver's head. We checked into the landmark Alfonso XIII Hotel and went straight to bed. I vaguely remember the hotel being pretty, but was too exhausted to care. Typical of jet lag, I woke up at about two in the morning, disoriented and a bit dizzy, and opened a window for some fresh air and . . . *Wow!*

I was overlooking the gardens of the Alcazar Palace, the royal residence of the Moorish rulers who invaded Spain over one thousand years ago. I could see the *Torre de Giralda*, a gorgeous Moorish belltower with a Catholic cathedral built around it. The old streetlamps glowed a beautiful amber hue. But it was the scent of orange blossoms, blooming all over the city, that struck some kind of curious cord within me.

I'm sure it was the jet lag, because I don't believe in reincarnation or past lives, but I experienced the most peculiar sense of déjà vu. It wasn't just the beautiful view; I've seen many. But there was something so distinctly comfortable and familiar about the place. I told myself, *Just in case I'm wrong about past lives, I must have lived here once, and I think I must have liked it very much.* Still today, orange blossoms are significant to me. I associate the fragrance with an impending change within me.

Normally, when filming in a foreign country, a producer will hire a location manager: someone familiar with the area, savvy with the customs, and so forth; someone who can take you to the exact places you're seeking. But John didn't much care for location managers. We had discovered many of them to be corrupt and self-serving, introducing you only to people who will give them kickbacks or favors of some kind.

The next morning, we went down to the lobby to arrange for a car and driver to begin our undesignated quest for shooting locations. The time in the lobby gave me a chance to admire the spectacular Alfonso XIII Hotel, which was built in the 1920s in classic Andalusian architecture, an exotic mixture of Spanish and Moorish. The hotel was used for many scenes in *Lawrence of Arabia*. I whined to John, "This is crazy! We should have hired somebody to take us around." Just then, we ran smack into Manolo, a local newspaper photographer who had heard that we'd checked into the hotel and had been waiting for us since the crack of dawn. He didn't speak English; we didn't speak Spanish. Normally, we avoided paparazzi at all cost. I generally consider them a vile pack of scavengers, an opinion borne from having found one staked out in the bathroom of my hotel room in Rome, in hopes of getting a picture of me on the toilet. Another time, I got a smashed nose from a camera being shoved in my face as an elevator door was closing.

But there was something different about Manolo. He was an impish little man who spoke a mile a minute while the concierge translated. When he learned why we were in town, he dashed to the phone and chattered some more in the fastest Spanish I've ever heard.

John was looking very smug, because he was right about not needing a location manager. I had the feeling that we were in an old Sydney Greenstreet movie and had just met the Sevillian Peter Lorre. Seville is a very social city where everybody knows everybody, and Manolo knew them all. He was connected, a discreet and loyal member of Seville society.

Within minutes, we were speeding down the highway through olive groves and bull ranches with Manolo, our new guide, and Miguel, our new driver. We were on our way to Jerez de la Frontera to visit the Royal Andalusian Riding School, where the beautiful girl rode those stallions in Vavra's book.

The school was on the grounds of a beautiful palace. The riding arena was a virtual cathedral for me, vaulted arches and all, every inch dedicated to worshiping the horse. We sat in the royal box and looked out at twelve of the most beautiful creatures I had ever seen. From the first moment I saw them, I knew I had found the horse from my childhood dream.

Alvaro Domecq, the master of the riding school, was introduced to us. He had a proud, almost arrogant bearing that I find irresistible in the Spanish horsemen. Alvaro is the most exciting man on a horse I have ever seen. Some may be more beautiful, some more technically correct, some more elegant, but no one is more exciting.

I was trying to be polite during the introduction and pay attention to our conversation with Alvaro, but I couldn't keep my eyes off the silvery white stallions in the arena below. Alvaro caught me sneaking peeks. He smiled and asked, "Which one would you care to ride?"

I truly thought he was joking. I'd learned enough about horses to know that you never let a stranger, or duffer, or dude, on such a well-trained horse. It's not fair to an animal that has reached such a high level of schooling and brilliance to have someone without finesse poking his sides and pulling on his mouth with the reins. But Alvaro insisted.

"Hmmmm . . . That one," I said, pointing to a stallion who was just as gorgeous as the others.

Alvaro called out something in Spanish. Everyone in the arena took notice, and the stallion was led away. We followed Alvaro outside to the front of the palace, where the stallion was waiting. Alvaro gave me a leg up, and there I was astride this gorgeous creature with its powerful, high-arching neck. I could feel that goofy grin spreading across my face, the same one from the faded photograph of me on my first pony ride. I tried to hold it back, because Manolo's shutter was motoring away on his camera, and I thought my stupid expression would ruin the photos. But the joy was stronger than my vanity; I couldn't help it.

Alvaro stood beside me and told me which cues to give the horse, all in Spanish, which was a problem for only about two min-utes. Horses are horses, and my brain quickly comprehended what Alvaro was telling me to do.

"Hold the reins like this," he said. "Put your weight here. Give the pressure of the legs just so . . . ."

I had no idea what I was asking the horse to do, but suddenly it was *dancing*, a movement called *passage*. I felt like I was floating! How could such a powerful creature be so light and elegant?

"Put your weight back a little and hold the reins just a little lower," Alvaro instructed.

The horse went into *levade*, my absolute favorite *Haute Ecole* (high school) movement. The horse rises up on its hind legs, but not nearly as high as when it rears. The horse was perfectly balanced with his impulsion generated by his hind legs. But he was restrained by the pressure of my legs. I could feel his hindquarters quivering beneath me.

That was all it took. I was hooked. Forever.

"Poor Niagara," Eleanor Roosevelt said when she saw Iguazu Falls in South America for the first time.

I was thinking about my poor horses, Houdini, Slick, and Kawaleer, back home. I truly loved them all. They were funny and affectionate, but there was something missing: a connection. This Andalusian stallion was something entirely different. I was (or most likely it was my vanity) relating in some unexplainably personal way to him. I was thrilled with the ride alone. But what really got to me most was this horse's brilliance, the noble expression in his eyes, and how hard he concentrated to perform the movements perfectly.

There was something more than just where my weight was positioned on his back, more than how I held the reins, more than how I applied pressure to his sides with my legs. I sensed that he was loving the work and enjoying me as much as I was enjoying him.

Of course, I took it all personally. Just as in my childhood dream, my conceit made me feel that this stallion preferred to be with me than another horse. But, then again, maybe there *was* something there. The Andalusian (or Lusitano, depending on which part of the Iberian Peninsula the horse comes from) has such a rich history. It is the oldest saddle horse known to man, prized by the Greeks, Phoenicians, and Romans for war. The horse ridden by the conquistadores when they conquered the Americas. Maybe this noble breed has evolved to be a bit more domesticated or *tuned-in* to man than others. Well . . . I like to think so.

Those days in Spain were divine, going from ranch to ranch, with Manolo leading the way. John found his beautiful locations, sparking ideas for scenes that would later be strung together into a screenplay. Meanwhile, I was riding every horse the Spaniards would let me get my leg over. And the Spaniards were most obliging. We met Robert Vavra, the author of the book—and dozens of others—that started our journey. Robert is an American adventurer, writer, and photographer who first came to southern Spain in the late 1950s and spent many days and good times with his literary friends Ernest Hemingway and James Michener. We share a love of the country's people and culture and horses and bulls. Today Robert is one of my closest friends.

It was at the Peralta ranch outside of Seville that I got into bullfighting. The brothers Angel and Rafael Peralta are legendary *rejoneadors*, or bullfighters on horseback. No, not *picadors*, the horsemen who jab the animal with lances (*pics*) to weaken it and slow it down before the final stage of the bullfight. The picadors' horses are covered with a mattresslike padding that protects the right flank, giving the bull something to get his horns into, while a *matador* (a bullfighter with a cape) studies the bravery of the bull. In *rejoneo*, the horse has no protection from the bull except for the brains and skills of the rider. The *rejoneador* cues the horse to perform all those beautiful Haute Ecole movements to entice the bull to charge. Then hopefully the horse will dodge, feint the charge, and evade the bull just in the nick of time.

Being an animal lover, I won't defend bullfighting. Hemingway himself said, "The bullfight is indefensible. You either like it or you don't." But at the same time, I won't judge a tradition that goes back thousands of years. From what I've been able to gather, knowing that history is political, bullfighting is rooted in bull worship going back to ancient Sumerian and Mesopotamian cultures. The bull represented the supreme symbol of strength and fertility. So it was only natural that ancient man would have to kill it. Bullfighting as we know it today is probably a holdover from the ancient Roman games. The caste mark of a gladiator was a pigtail, similar to the ones matadors wear.

I recently asked Robert Vavra at dinner, "What is it about bullfighting that captivates me? Is it because I also like so many contact sports, like boxing?"

"The bullfight is a tragic art in which the bull almost always dies," he said. "It's not a sport or a contest between two more or less evenly matched opponents. The bull weighs a ton and is armed with horns. The man doesn't weigh two hundred pounds and is armed only with his intelligence. The only contest is between the man and himself, between the man and his own fear."

"But I love animals," I said. "Why can I accept the killing of a bull?"

"It's not about the bull," Robert replied. "Why do aficionados cheer the matador? Because he stands still in the face of death, an act of bravery of which they would be incapable. Why does the crowd jeer the matador if he doesn't stand still? Because they see in him what their own reaction would be if they were alone in the ring, armed with a mere piece of cloth in the face of death."

"But the innocent bull?"

"To compare a fighting bull to a domestic bull that we farm for food is like comparing the great white shark to a goldfish. Far crueler is the life of our beef cattle who stand their whole lives—sometimes knee-deep in their own feces—smelling blood and death, their eyes glazed over with fear. The brave bull has a gloriously free life: green pastures of great expanse, birds, butterflies, flowers, social interaction with his fellow bulls, the sun, the moon. Give me the liberty of the life of the fighting bull and give me his death, not the existence and end of what goes into a hamburger."

My very first day riding the Peralta horses, I went into the ring with a young female calf. I rode a stunning gray stallion named Bohemio, who was fast and furious. I didn't cue Bohemio with my hands or legs or even by shifting my weight. He was far too sensitive and reactive for that. If I had pulled on his reins even slightly, as I would normally cue a horse to stop, he would go over backward. I had to consciously leave my hands and legs out of it. If I wanted to turn, I would think *Turn!*—barely glancing in the direction I wanted to go—and we would be turning.

As the calf entered the ring, she ran around looking for something, *anything* to kill. First she looked at my horse, then at me. It was the same look that Dandy Lion had when he tried to take off my shoulder during the filming of *Tarzan*. Clearly, she wanted me dead.

The calf dropped her head to charge me, and Angel rode out in front and took her charge. For only a moment I thought, *What the hell am I doing here?!* I still couldn't understand most of what Angel and Rafael said to me. But we had developed our own code of communication during the day. They would say, "*Mira*, Bo!" Then they'd do something spectacular on the horse and say, "*Vale!*" "Do it," and I would blindly try to do whatever they said. Unlike my day with Alvaro, who told me every single cue and move to make, it was strictly through visualization and imitation that I was riding these magnificent horses and making moves that I'd never dreamed of.

I'd never seen such horsemanship in my life. Angel is the most beautiful, elegant man on a horse, and Rafael is funny and talented and loved by the crowd when he fights bulls. Angel taunted the calf to the other side of the ring and instructed, "Venga ["Come here"], Bo!" I looked up at John. He nodded *the nod*. The nod that told me, "You can do it." The nod that always gave me confidence.

I swear that Bohemio could feel my heart pounding as I prepared to commit myself. He gathered and collected himself into such a tight wad of explosive energy that something very exceptional happened. The horse was completely under me, totally trusting of me, that when I wanted to stay just a little longer in front of the charge, Bohemio stood. Bold and brave without the slightest inclination to bolt. I realized then that Bohemio would stand and be gored if I had asked him too. That's weighty stuff.

So I agree that bullfighting is a brutal, gruesome slaughter of an innocent animal. For sure, humankind has evolved into a more civilized creature. I say *more* civilized because we unquestionably love our football, boxing, car races, and all the sports that still fascinate us with the drama and the blood of the arena. It's all a big dilemma for me.

I was having such a good time riding horses and making new friends and preparing the film *Bolero* that I didn't give much thought to the part I would play. The role of Ayre McGillivary was written just for me, so the character was comfy. When the first day's shooting arrived, I was a little nervous. I had never been nervous before. My first scene was difficult, with lots of dialogue and animation. We were shooting nights. It was cold. Let's see . . . Can I think up any more excuses for why I stank as an actress? I reeked!

Our crew included a dialogue coach named Mickey Knox. His job was to help the Spanish actors with their accents and to help them understand dialogue. Mickey is also a veteran actor: in fact, he played John's brother in *Knock on Any Door* in 1949, among other roles. But in the early 1950s, at the height of Senator Joseph McCarthy's public witch hunt for alleged Communist sympathizers, Mickey left Hollywood for Rome, disgusted with America and friend turning against friend. John and Mickey had remained good friends over the years, and we hired him for every one of our films.

After the first take, John turned to Mickey. "What the fuck was *that?*"

"She's just nervous, John," Mickey replied.

After the fifth take, John came over to me. I was sitting in the backseat of a vintage Rolls-Royce. He tried to cheer me up and cajole me out of my state of utter terror. I didn't know what was happening to me. I may have been bad in scenes before, but I'd never suffered stage fright!

We tried again. Poor George Kennedy, who was playing my chauffeur, was so embarrassed for me. He sat frozen in the front seat and never said a word. He must have known what I was going through, because if he had said anything—even a word of encouragement!—I think I would have lost it for sure. The sixth take was just as bad as the first, and I was on the verge of becoming a blubbering idiot.

I heard John say to Mickey, "I can't do anything with her. I give up!"

"John, you can't give up!" Mickey said. "Go talk to her."

"I can't talk to her, *you* talk to her. You direct the scene, and I'll shoot it. You tell me when to roll and when to cut."

Mickey walked over to the car and tried to cheer me up, but I was too far gone for that. So he went back to stand beside the camera. "Okay," he said, "roll." Sweet Mickey started yelling out everything I should be thinking about in the scene. After screaming and yelling and jumping up and down like a cheerleader to wind me up, he shouted, "Action!"

I blurted out the dialogue, with just enough of Mickey's energy channeling through me, and I was over my terror. Stage fright is nasty.

Golan and Globus, the Israeli producers, left us alone a little *too* much and never sent the money on time. They always had a ridiculous reason as to why. That left me and my American Express card to keep production going while we waited for funds. I'm a big believer in maintaining a paper trail, so I have a big book full of telegrams and letters threatening them for breach of contract. But eventually the money would come. John could then calm down, and we could continue filming. On the last day's work, the cousins tried to give me Bohemio as a peace treaty, but I wouldn't accept it. (Silly me and my scruples; I loved that horse.)

Postproduction was fraught with even more problems. While waiting once again for money to be transferred, we ended up losing control of the film and never got paid.

Cannon Films reedited the love scenes, making them longer. We tried to fight the cousins in the press, which was foolish, although *60 Minutes* was good enough to let me say my piece and show my paper trail of innocence. But we knew it was time to hang up the gloves when Menahem Golan held a press conference at which he threatened: "They love that ranch, and ve vill take it away!" He went on to call John a "demon" and claimed, "The Dereks have made the film too sexy!" Golan's statements were just too juicy. In defending ourselves, we would just be giving the media more ammunition with which to assail us.

Oh, well. Chalk it up to a good learning experience. Keep your mouth shut when it comes to the press. And terms like *paper trails, breach of contract, force majeure, payment schedules,* and all the new legal knowledge and vocabulary I had learned during my years of major motion picture making taught me the most valuable lesson of all: It's all nonsense. He who has the most wins.

FOURTEEN

And God took a handful of southerly wind, blew his
breath over it and created the horse.

—BEDOUIN LEGEND

In 1983, upon returning to the ranch from Spain, I started a small horse-breeding business, specializing in Spanish and Andalusian, and Portuguese Lusitano horses. *Business* is probably the wrong word. As my friend CiCi says, "The only way to make a small fortune in the horse business is to start with a large one." My horses *almost* paid for themselves, which put me way ahead of most people who have the same compulsion to spend their lives with equines.

I dove headfirst into the world of animal reproduction with my new mentor, Dr. Doug Herthel, a brilliant veterinarian and good friend. I had six stallions standing at stud but only four broodmares. My business was directed at selling the unique DNA contained in my stallions' sperm.

My own stable of stallions. It was thrilling. Stallions are noisy and showy, always strutting from here to there. They could never just take a leisurely walk to a paddock. Oh, no! There might be a mare watching, so they must always look impressive. I charged a lot of money to allow customers—the mares—to spend a moment with one of my beautiful males. I advertised my stallions' merits and physical attributes shamelessly in glossy magazines. It's funny that all of this is accepted and legal in the horse world but considered depraved and amoral in the human one.

By the time a stallion in the wild *covers* (copulates with) a mare, he has had a certain sexual education. He's seen sex from the time that, as a ten-day-old foal, he stood to the side while his sire covered his dam. Today, very few horses are brought up in a herd and family unit. Like zoo-bred animals, they are often awkward, ineffective breeders.

Ramon Becerra let me know whenever one of the girls came into heat. Everything came to a stop, because there is only a small window of opportunity for a mare to conceive. I would immediately run down to the barn to prepare the mare. I can't tell you how many times I might be talking to a friend when I'd get the heads-up from Ramon. "Sorry, got to go!" I'd say. "We have to breed a mare!"

"You mean right now, right here?" my friends would say.

"Yes, down by the barn."

"Umm, can I watch?"

"Sure!"

First thing I'd do is clean her up and wrap her tail, so that the stallion would not be hurt by one of her nasty tail hairs, which God must have put there to keep the numbers of stallions in proportion to the herd. If the chosen stallion were Mouro, it would be an easy cover. Mouro was primitive and had probably spent his early life in a herd. He was proud and approached everything in life with gusto. His athletic ability made him a good lover, and he was always kind to the mares. He stayed cool and composed until the time was right and then went about the breeding like a pro.

Centauro, on the other hand, was awkward and particular. He might get overexcited and miss the target. Or he would scream in frustration and sometimes nip the mare. Ramon often needed to assist him. Centauro absolutely hated "Blue Dummy," a big, long, padded hulk that somewhat resembled a horse's torso. We used Blue Dummy to collect semen that was promptly FedExed to breeders with ready mares. But because Centauro would refuse to "breed" Blue Dummy, we would have to bring a real mare alongside the dummy. Then, at the last moment, we would redirect Centauro to the collecting container. Mouro, of course, *loved* Blue Dummy and would come flying out of his trailer fully erect and calling out to "her."

In a live cover, my job was to hold the mare and give her support, while the spectacular stallion was led out of the barn and shown her hindquarters. Some mares, even though they were at the peak of estrus and in serious heat, would get nervous. I would talk to them, stroke them, try to calm them. Standing by the mare's head, with the sight of a stallion rearing up over my head to mount the mare, is something so beautifully breathtaking. As I would stroke her neck and lean into her just a little to help her support the stallion's weight, I could, at a certain point, see in the soft expression in her eyes that she didn't need me anymore.

When the covering was over, the stallion would usually stay on top of the mare for a few moments, then rise up and roll off her rump.

My friends were always truly impressed with the event, and had something profound to say, like a breathy "Wow!"

That would be the first and last time the stallion would see the mare, unless he was chosen to breed her again the following year.

Then a long wait would begin. Gestation in horses is 355 days. My favorite broodmare, Celosa (Spanish for "jealous"), is a beautiful, powerful, yet feminine Spanish mare. In the last month of her pregnancy, Celosa would get so huge and uncomfortable. Her enormous belly would sway from side to side as she walked. She would always nicker as I approached, asking her, "How are you today, *guapa?*"

She would gently greet me with her soft muzzle and smell my face, then put her chin on my shoulder and let out a long groan as if to tell me how miserable she was. She'd stay there resting on me with her breath in my ear until she fell asleep. Her chin would get very heavy, but I wouldn't dare move. Eventually, a sound or a fly bite would startle her awake, and she would let out another moan.

The mare will foal tonight, I thought one night while checking on Celosa. Her teats were running with milk, and the muscles around her tail were as slack as Jell-O. It was a full moon—very auspicious. I knew I wouldn't be getting any sleep. I asked Ramon to watch her until midnight, when I would take over. Then I went to the house to cook dinner. I had become a pretty good cook by this time and was making a pizza for some good friends. Although pizza is one of my specialties, my pies have never been reliable. Luckily, the dough rose perfectly that night and the pizza was a good one. Just as I was bringing dessert to the table, Ramon called. "Celosa just broke her water," he said.

I told my friends to help themselves to dessert, but I was going to foal out my mare. They all got very excited and ran out with me to the grassy foaling pen. Most farms foal in a large stall bedded deep with straw. But Doug Herthel had told me that the best place is outdoors on grass, where the sunlight prevents the mold and bacteria found in most stalls from forming. John adamantly disagreed when the nights were cold, but I held tough. Doug was my guide, mentor, and god, so we always foaled outside.

By the time I made it to the pen, Celosa was starting to go down to the ground, and I could see a little hoof protruding from under her tail.

"*Guapa,*" I whispered to her.

She nickered a stressful welcome to me, then went down heavily. I stroked her head while she had strong contractions. Ramon said the head was out, so I went down to her tail and grabbed the foal's forelegs and helped pull as Celosa pushed. After a few efforts and loud groans from Celosa, the foal's shoulders and chest were out. I went to Celosa's head; she put her head in my lap and took a little rest. Then she raised her head. As I went back to the foal, she gave the last pushes. The foal slid out easily into my arms.

I began to dry the foal with towels because it was a cold night. I noticed that it was a filly, and she was shivering. Eventually, Celosa stood up and broke the umbilical cord. I quickly doused the stem with iodine and gave the foal a quick enema, which, understandably, offended the foal no end. Celosa was nickering to her foal, which begins the bonding process between mare and foal. The sweet little foal let out a shrill whinny, and Celosa licked her all over until she was dry.

Part of my duty as midwife was to tie up the amniotic sac until Celosa passed the afterbirth. If she should step on the sac, it could tear her uterus. Easier said than done! The sac is a man-sized, slippery, slimy mass dripping with blood and amniotic fluid. Every horseperson has their own way of tying up the sac. On the night in question, my method wasn't working very well. A girlfriend, who had come out to watch, offered to help, but got a little queasy at having to touch it.

"I don't think I can do this, Bo," she said, grimacing.

I looked up at her, all covered in fluids, and said, "Fine, but think of it this way: We pay two dollars apiece for those little vials of placenta extract to condition our hair. Here we have the real thing!"

There is a method of imprinting accepted as fact in the horse world: If a human spends the first fifteen minutes with the foal, before it rises to its feet, you can influence how it will perceive humans in the future. You will also influence how events will or will not frighten a horse throughout its life. With this in mind, people touch the foal all over, jingle bits and tack near the ears for the foal to hear, even run the electric clippers over the body that will later be used to trim the ears and the muzzle hairs.

I've never quite bought into the benefits of this method. The first twenty minutes of the foal's life is when the mare imprints her voice and smell with her foal, crucial to survival in the wild. I found that my interference only confused the foal. When it finally got to its feet, it would follow me and try to suckle *me*, making the mare very anxious and nervous.

Once Celosa's sac was secure, I left the pen and watched nature at work by the light of the full moon. My girlfriend suggested we name her Luna. Little Luna put her head down and took a short nap. She awoke and whinnied for her mother, and Celosa came and touched muzzles with her. Luna struggled to rise on wobbly legs and finally collapsed into a little heap of exhaustion. This would go on many times throughout the night until the filly could finally stand long enough to find a teat and suckle, getting the all-important colostrum, the first milk that would protect her from infections.

It was after midnight once Luna had nursed. Then we all went to bed. I awoke at dawn and looked out the window. A heavy fog had come in, and I couldn't see the foaling pen at all. I went out to find Celosa down, sleeping with her filly at her side. Celosa lifted her head when she heard me coming. I went to her side and whispered, "*Guapa*, how do you feel this morning? You have such a beautiful baby!"

Celosa moaned and swung her big, beautiful head into my lap. I stroked her face and neck for the longest time. Suddenly, Luna's head popped up and whinnied. Celosa didn't even lift her head; just made a low rumbling noise. Luna jumped up, her legs much more steady than when we had left her. She startled when she realized I was there. But curiosity got the better of her, and she clumsily made her way over to me and tentatively sniffed my face and hair with her sweet little foal breath. Luna whinnied again and stomped her front foreleg. She was hungry. Celosa just rumbled something in horse and opened her legs slightly so that the filly could nurse. There I was sitting in the thick fog, stroking Celosa's neck and chest while her filly spread her long forelegs and bent her head down to nurse. I could hear the suckling sounds. *How does life get any better than this?* I thought to myself.

My way of bonding with a foal took a lot of time. I liked to take a chair and a book and go out to the pasture. Celosa would doze on my shoulder a while and then go on to graze. If her foal was skittish, which some are just born to be, just like children, I would avoid eye contact, ignore the foal, and just sit and read my book aloud. Foals are so curious by nature; eventually she would approach me, then get scared and run away, bucking. Pretty soon, the foal would start chewing on my hair and striking me with her forelegs and climb on top of me, just as she would one of her foal buddies in the pasture. That's when I would start to touch her and earn her trust. I think the fact that the foals heard my voice for hours at a time while they were young has helped me to calm them throughout their lives. But the electric clippers still scare the shit out of them the first time!

I don't breed horses anymore. I suppose I suffered from a condition many mothers contract: giving birth to the messiah child. One day I looked around and saw twenty-six horses on the ranch, and they were all mine! I'd kept every foal I bred and adopted any poor sod with a *Black Beauty* story that came my way. The ranch was only forty-six acres, not nearly big enough to support a herd that size. The land was overgrazed, and the fences were being pushed over by the sheer horseflesh.

I set aside my emotions and entered the most difficult part of the horse business: selling. Actually accepting money for all those little princes and princesses that I had helped foal and raise. Unfortunately, not everyone who came to see my perfect standards of equus felt the same way I did. I might have overreacted a bit the first time a potential customer said something like "I don't like the way she moves. She's too round."

"You must not be familiar with the breed!" I insisted. "Her movement is perfect! If you want a daisy-cutter, you should get a warm-blood."

I remember wanting to hit him.

My sister Kerry, who was still working for us after ten years, pulled me aside and suggested that she and John show the horses from then on. Eventually, she had to keep John out of it too. Whenever a young woman—usually pretty—fell in love with one of our horses, he would just *give* the animal to her.

On her own, Kerry did a great job of finding good homes for all of my foals, which was of course the priority for me. Today, years later, I still get letters and photos from happy customers, telling me how one of my horses has changed their lives. This part of it makes it all worthwhile. But the other side of horse breeding—the ever-present specter that potential buyers might not treat my horses as well as I did—made me stop breeding altogether.

With all of my sales, I insisted on one condition: that I could buy back the horse should the customer not want to keep it, for whatever reason. A year after selling Luna, I found her photo in a horse-trader publication; she was for sale. Kerry immediately called the buyer. The buyer said that she was embarrassed to let us know that she couldn't keep the horse any longer. But not to worry, things had changed since she put in the ad, and she was keeping Luna after all.

It was then that I realized, albeit a little late, that I was responsible for some two dozen little lives. As we all know from famous literature written about horses, like *Black Beauty*, *Smokey*, and *The Godolphin Arabian*, the life of a horse can be so tragic. Not ten miles from my ranch was a sales yard where a rancher's old, lame, or just excess horses were auctioned off every Thursday afternoon. They were then shipped in cattle trucks to Canada for slaughter.

I had stupidly, arrogantly assumed that mine would be different, *because* they were mine. Of course, I was wrong. So I'll never breed horses again.

FIFTEEN

Horse sense is what a horse has that keeps him
from betting on people.

—W. C. FIELDS

One of the natural consequences of fame is that you can become a target of con men. A charlatan can pull off fantastic scams if he can associate, even in the tiniest way, with a movie star (or the CIA).

It was as if John and I put out some kind of scent to bring them in. It wasn't because we were so independent that we were susceptible or exposed to cons. There was a time when we had the proper Hollywood entourage: buffers to protect us and do background checks before someone was allowed in our presence. At one point, it even cost thousands of dollars just to have a "face-to-face" with the Dereks. You would think that making people pay money would weed out the crooks. But it didn't.

In 1985 Marty Baum called to say that a brilliant young financier named Bill wanted to meet us. He would pay ten thousand dollars just for the opportunity. No obligations. Marty had checked this Bill out and found that he had graduated top of his class at Stanford Business School, and he was all the talk at a big investment firm.

We had a meeting with Bill at which he presented an offer to make three films for seven million dollars each. He had a group of investors that wanted to get into the film business. It sounded good to us, so we made the deal. Bill was a very energetic, enthusiastic, and naive young man. He immediately fell under John's spell and hung on to his every word. As the particulars of the deal were being worked out among the attorneys, which took about three weeks, Bill would call almost every night. He would pump John for information about films, distribution, and the old days of Hollywood.

It didn't take long to notice that Hollywood was going to Bill's head. He was getting cocky. John used to tease him about becoming a big shot. One night Bill called and bragged about all the deals he was making, saying that he was getting the biggest stars and directors. John warned him not to go too fast. "This business is full of pricks," John said. "The worst part is not that they will steal your money. That you can handle. But they will make a fool of you. I've seen it so many times, and being made a fool will drive you crazy for the rest of your life."

Bill, already quite arrogant, said, "Don't worry about me. I'm the new whiz kid in town, the young genius."

"You stupid son of a bitch, don't you listen to anything I say?" John said. "I can see you now, up in Silicon Valley, naked in front of a mirror, playing with yourself, saying, 'I'm a mogul! I'm a mogul!'"

Bill immediately got very contrite and apologized. "You're right, John. You're right. I got carried away. Thank you, John. Thank you so much. Thank you for setting me straight! I want to be strong. I want to be more like you, John!"

"Don't be like me," John said. "Stand up and be a man. Be like John Wayne, for Christ's sake! Be the Duke!"

Bill got so excited. "Yes, John, you're right!" he said. "I will be a man."

From then on Bill's nickname was Duke.

This happened over and over again. There was always a young hotshot who would attach himself to John, and the more truthful, insulting, and offensive John got, the more they would love it. It must be the whole alpha-male thing. John would bite, and they would roll over and pee on themselves!

One night Bill called and told me that the investors wanted to meet us. But, he added, we would have to sign a letter of confidentiality first.

"Why?"

"They must keep their privacy," Bill said.

"Why?" I asked again. "Better we not meet them at all. Just send the money according to the contract."

"No, you have to meet them, they insist," said Bill. "But the time and place must absolutely be kept secret until the last second."

"Bill, this is not part of the deal, and now I'm getting spooked," I said. "What could they possibly have to hide?"

"I really can't say any more about it on the phone," said Bill.

"Bill, what are you on?" I asked. Of course, everybody was on drugs in the mid-1980s. "You're acting paranoid. If you're straight, just go away and find somebody else to have your secret meetings with. I want nothing to do with it." With that, I hung up the phone.

Bill called back the next day. This time he got John on the phone. He said that someone representing the investors wanted to meet with us. Just a social call. John said, "Okay. No secret shit?"

"No, John, no secret shit." Bill giggled. He loved swearing in front of John.

On the nonsecret night at the nonsecret time, Bill brought a man named Ronald Rewald to the ranch. We had a houseguest with us, Claude, the jet-setter who knew everybody who was anybody. We thought it might be a good idea for her to be in the meeting as a witness. Rewald was an attractive young man, and we liked him immediately—something that I would later take as a bad sign. After a few minutes of socializing, John said, "What's this shit about having to sign a confidentiality letter to meet you?"

Rewald assured us that there was nothing illegal about the investors, but their identities were just . . . "sensitive."

"That sounds like a bunch of crap," said John.

"Let me be frank," Rewald said.

"What have you been doing so far, lying to us all night?" John said. He always saw red when someone said "Let me be frank" or "Let me be honest with you."

"No, John, let me start over," said Rewald. "I represent a group of foreign investors who want to get money out of their country and into the United States."

"It's not illegal for foreigners to invest in this country," said John.

"No, you're right, but some of the countries don't want the money leaving," Rewald said. "I assure you that the investors involved are all friendly to the United States. The money is good for our economy, and as a result, the U.S. sort of looks the other way."

"Go on," said John.

"There are many big families who want to get their money out of countries with unstable governments," Rewald said. "Like the Gandhis of India or the Marcoses of the Philippines. Or Enrique Zobel, one of the richest men in the world. He's the chairman of the Bank of the Philippine Islands."

"Is any of this money from drugs or prostitution?" John asked. "I don't want anything to do with that."

Rewald assured us that the money was not from anything illegal or immoral. He was a devout Catholic with five kids, he said. He would never do anything to put his children in jeopardy.

We talked about the film projects and said good night. As soon as they were out the door, John, Claude, and I looked at one another. I know my eyes were huge. Claude said that she knew most of these families and had heard of these kinds of deals. She would make some calls in the morning. John said that I should call a friend of ours who had obscure connections with the Federal Bureau of Investigation.

The next morning I called our friend and told him about our meeting. He thought that it could be for real. Then he asked for the name of the investor liaison.

"Ronald Rewald," I said.

The friend practically screamed, "Don't you read the papers? Ron Rewald is being tried as the biggest con man of the decade, maybe the century. It's the biggest case since Nugan Hand.

"You idiot!" my friend continued. "This guy could be dangerous. Jesus, didn't you see him on the evening news a couple of months ago? He was found in a hotel room in Hawaii with his wrists slit and blood all over the walls. He says that he was an operative for the Central Intelligence Agency. There's a whole First Amendment issue over this guy. President Reagan just sealed some records by executive order. It's a big deal. I'll call a friend who's kind of connected to the CIA and ask him to call you immediately. Tell this guy everything; you can trust him. I've known him since we were both mercenaries in Africa."

Now, *that's* a recommendation that'll make you feel better!

I spoke with the CIA-connected friend. He said that I should call the FBI immediately. Did I know anyone? If not, he said, he could give me the name of an agent. But, he added, he'd rather not get involved. "The FBI has had thirty agents on Ron Rewald for over a year and a half," the man said. It was a huge investigation.

I told him that John and I had met some agents from the L.A. office. They were working on the U. S. side of a 1981 case in which a British teenager fired six blanks at Queen Elizabeth II; in his pocket was a note he'd written to *me* so *I* was questioned. The CIA man said, "Perfect. Call them right away."

"And," he added, "I'd appreciate it if you don't mention that we spoke."

The FBI agents I had met before were not in, so I spoke to another instead. I didn't like him from the start. Nevertheless, I outlined for him the deal we were involved in and explained that "a man" had said that money would be coming from various countries. Not much reaction from the agent. He asked who the man was.

"Ronald Rewald," I said.

That piqued his interest. The agent asked me to elaborate on some of the things that Rewald had told us about the investors. Claude was in the room, listening to my side of the conversation.

"Did Mr. Rewald mention any other names?" the agent asked.

"Yes. He said that one of the investors was the Sultan of Brunei."

"*No,*" Claude interrupted, "he said that he played polo with the Sultan. The Sultan was not one of the investors."

I asked the agent to hold on a minute. John agreed with my version of the story, but Claude shook her head. "I know exactly what he said," she insisted, "because I have it on tape."

"What do you mean you have it on tape?" asked John.

"Well, you got this new little tape recorder, and you know, John, anything you get, I have to have. So I thought I would try it out. During the meeting, I had it between my knees under my skirt. When you talked, I turned my knees toward you; and when Rewald talked, I turned my knees toward him. It worked perfectly!"

"Claude, I think that's illegal!" I said. "You can't secretly tape someone."

The agent had obviously overheard us, despite my having covered the receiver with my hand. "Excuse me, did I hear that there is a tape?" he asked.

"Yes, I guess there is, but I didn't know anything about it," I said.

"Where are you calling from, Mrs. Derek?" he asked.

"I'm at my home, about a hundred miles north of L.A."

"We can be there in two and a half hours," he said. "Will you be available to meet with us?"

"Yes, sure," I said.

Claude, a very emotional woman, went into a panic that she might be in trouble. She got on the phone to her attorney, who had been one of President Kennedy's legal advisors, to find out whether she should turn over the tape. By the time the two agents arrived, Claude had made up her mind not to turn over the tape unless she received immunity from the court. The agents assured her that wouldn't be a problem.

They questioned us all for a couple of hours. At one point, one agent asked, "Mr. Derek, do you think Mr. Rewald has the money that he claims?"

"Yes, I do," John said.

"Then why did you call us?" the agent asked. "That would be a lot of money for you. Why didn't you just go forward with the deal?"

John, highly insulted, said, "Fuck you!"

"I have to assume that for you to pass up such a lucrative deal, you must want some kind of reward," the agent said.

"Fuck you and get out!" John said.

They left. By the end of the day, the agents that I had originally wanted to talk to called and apologized for the ungracious agent. He asked if we would continue to help them. "Yes, but only with you, no other agents," I said. "John liked both of you, but he won't put up with anyone like the last guy."

We met with the new agents. Now it was our turn to get information about Rewald. It seems that he had an investment firm in Honolulu called Bishop, Baldwin, Rewald, Dillingham, and Wong. I knew some of those names belonged to the oldest, most powerful families in Hawaii. Problem was, he had just used their names to make it appear as though these families were part of the company. They weren't. Rewald bilked hundreds of people out of twenty million dollars. The victims included a former *Playboy* Playmate who was now paralyzed and had a six-year-old son to raise. He finally got caught when an IRS agent, who happened to be a neighbor, grew suspicious after seeing the Rewald children being chauffeured to school in a limousine.

"But what about his connection with the CIA?" John asked.

"Well, at one point, Rewald's office was used as a CIA address, a mailbox," the agent explained. "Nothing more than that."

"Then why would President Reagan seal some documents?"

"Rewald copied some of the mail before sending it on. Some top-secret missile designs ended up in his son's school science project."

A lot of facts didn't quite add up about Rewald. His big mistake with us, the agents said, was that the judge had specifically ordered him not to conduct any more investment business while he awaited trial. They asked if the special prosecutor could come out from Washington, D.C., next week and grant Claude immunity for her tape as well as obtain a statement from me. Also, if we were given immunity, would we continue to talk with Rewald and tape the conversations? John didn't think we should, but I wanted to. Although Rewald had never done anything harmful to us, except waste our time, I thought it was the right thing to do. I also have to admit that it was exciting. John said that I should be the only one involved, just in case it ever led to giving testimony. He was too hot-tempered for that.

The agents gave me some comically primitive equipment for recording telephone calls.

"Is this the best you have?" I asked. "I've got better that a journalist from the *National Enquirer* gave me." So I used my own wiring equipment.

I never spoke to Rewald about the trial; never got his side of the story. He didn't bring it up, which I consider a gigantic deception. He probably thought he'd struck gold when he met us. We must have been the only two chumps on earth who didn't know about his trial, enabling him to continue his scheme.

John and I made sure never to miss the evening news now. One night we watched in disbelief as anchorman Peter Jennings introduced a special two-part report on Ron Rewald and the CIA. One source, interviewed on camera, claimed that Rewald was a deep-cover agent for the organization. The report further stated that the CIA had hired a hit man to assassinate Rewald. This claim prompted director William Casey to file a formal complaint with the Federal Communications Commission. Jack Anderson, the syndicated newspaper columnist, ran stories about the case for twenty-seven straight weeks. I called Jack and explained my involvement. He warned me to be careful. In fact, Anderson himself had just received a death threat, and he believed Rewald to be highly dangerous.

Whatever the truth was, I reasoned that Rewald shouldn't be going against the judge's orders and continue the same business practices—using the same names, even—for which he had been charged with fraud. The truth was the truth, and I was only telling what had happened.

God, it was scary recording Ron Rewald! My heart pounded so hard, that I'm surprised he didn't catch on. The agents had told me to be natural. By no means should I try to entrap Rewald; I was to just talk to him about the films and production and anything else that

I would normally discuss regarding a film agreement. I know I was overly nice; my voice used to get high-pitched. I would sign off like he was my favorite person in the world.

By the time the special prosecutor came out to the ranch, I had a nice set of tapes for him, but nothing that I thought contained a smoking gun. It turned out that Claude had clenched her knees together too tightly just when Rewald got to the most incriminating part of her tape, so you couldn't hear it. That made my statement all the more important. I had discussed it with John, and he insisted that if I did this, I should sign only that "the above is true to the best of my knowledge." He told me not to get talked into anything else. That made sense to me. The special prosecutor was young and really cocky; John disliked him instantly. My husband stood at the back of our office with the FBI agents while I went over my statement for hours with the prosecutor, who kept trying to twist my words. When we finally got through the statement, feeling it was accurate, I told him that I wouldn't swear it was the truth—only to the best of my knowledge. He flipped out and said that I had wasted his time.

"It's worthless," he said of the statement. I apologized but said that was the only way I would sign it.

John, who had stayed out of it all day, whispered to the agents that if "the little, cocky shit" didn't back off, he was going to shoot him. "Go ahead, we'll back you," they replied. "We hate him!"

In the end, I held tough. The agents left with my tapes, Claude's tape, and my statement.

About a week later, they called, absolutely ecstatic about their day in court. It seems that somehow the special prosecutor had given the tapes to the judge. When Rewald's lawyers found out, they insisted on hearing them. In his chambers, the judge said that if they insisted, he would make the tapes public. And, he added, they, the lawyers, didn't want what was on those tapes to become public record. I still don't think there was anything really incriminating on them. But the lawyers dropped the claim to the tapes. The trial continued, with Rewald's lawyers believing that their client had made damaging statements to me.

I never did have to testify. My signed statement was strong enough, and in the end, Rewald was found guilty. At the sentencing the judge said: "You have been found guilty by a jury of your peers. You won't be there when Debbie [Rewald's daughter] grows into a young woman. You'll never see Jeff [his son] play another game of football. Mr. Rewald, you will not be there when your daughter Buffy graduates. You won't be there when your daughter Pamela gets married. You won't be there when your son Jim has his first child. You will never again enjoy your wife's company and comfort as husband and wife. I'm sentencing you to a term of eighty years."

One newspaper carried this headline MAN WHO TRIES TO CHEAT DEREKS GETS PRISON. The article said that my statement sealed the case against Rewald, whom the paper called the greatest con man of the decade. Rewald sent us Christmas cards from his cell at the Terminal Island correctional facility. Once he included a note asking that I reevaluate my statement so that he might get parole. I don't think so.

I felt awful for Bill, though. True to John's prediction, he never got over it. The young "genius" had left his job with the big investment company and had put everything into his partnership with Ronald Rewald. His empire crumbled with Rewald's conviction. He was no longer the mogul, just another young hotshot who blew it.

He did, however, manage to sue us for $120 million. For some reason or other, he blamed his demise on us. One day at dawn, I woke up and looked out over the ranch. It was really foggy, but I could see a white car parked just outside the courtyard gate. There was a man inside, his head hanging limply out the window, as if he were dead. I woke John, and we pulled out the binoculars. I called

Claude, who was still a houseguest; she wasn't expecting anyone, either. John grabbed a gun and went out to see who it was, accompanied by the dogs. I watched from my window as John woke up the man in the car. Claude joined them, and they all started walking toward the house.

Shit! It was Bill.

I went down to the kitchen. There they were, sitting and talking. John had this bemused expression on his face. Finally, he said to Bill, "Well, tell Bo then."

Bill went into this story about how he was afraid for his life. All hell had broken loose when Rewald went to prison. The Soviet KGB was after him. He was afraid for his mother, who was on her way to see an eye surgeon in Chicago. Bill claimed to have received an anonymous call that his mother would be killed at the doctor's office. His old girlfriend was after him. He claimed she had joined a witches' coven and kept men's body parts in jars.

"Hold on a minute," I interrupted. "What are you doing here?"

"Bo, I didn't know where to go!" said Bill. "You and John are the only ones who have been honest with me throughout this whole disaster."

"Bill, you're suing us for $120 million dollars, and you're costing us a fortune in legal fees!" I said.

"I know, but I've come here for sanctuary!"

"Well, you can't get it here," I snapped. "I don't want your problems with the KGB *or* the witch."

John, meanwhile, was smiling and enjoying this way too much.

"Bo, please!" Bill pleaded. "They'll kill me!"

"Okay, Bill, I'll go over to the computer and type up a quitclaim for you to sign dropping the lawsuit," I said. "Then we'll talk."

"Bo, I can't do that!" Bill protested. "I can't tell you why. But I can't."

"Then get out of here," I said. "I hope the KGB *does* kill you."

"I can't drop the lawsuit," Bill repeated.

He started to say that there was still some question of John not telling the truth. Our dining room chairs swiveled and tipped back, which was good for having long meaningful conversations after dinner, John had said when he designed them. That's when I went crazy. I leapt at Bill and started hitting him as hard as I could.

"How dare you come into our home and ask for help!" I screamed. "I hate you! You have ruined our life for the last six months! And now you accuse John of lying? You just said that he was the only honest man you know! I'll kill you myself!"

Bill, pinned back in the chair, was looking up in astonishment at this screaming banshee sitting on his chest, pummeling him.

"Bo! Bo! Stop, please! Ow! Ow! That hurts! Please, Bo, stop!"

John finally pulled me off him, laughing so hard at my violent outburst that he couldn't speak. Bill was a big guy. Granted, he was soft, but big. I guess I caught him off guard. Claude, too, was hysterical. She escorted Bill outside to talk to him. John and I spied on them through the binoculars. I could see her scolding Bill, who looked like a little boy in big trouble. After a half hour or so, Claude came back into the house and said that I should type up the quitclaim.

"Thanks, Claude, but it won't hold up," I said. "After I attacked him like that, I think it would be called 'under duress.'"

"So what, darling? We'll worry about duress later. I can get him to sign it." Which she did. After Bill had left, I asked Claude how she'd gotten him to sign the quitclaim.

"I told him that you and John really do care about him," she replied. "And that John will still be his friend."

Bill dropped the lawsuit, and we never saw or spoke to him again. Tragically, last I heard, Bill had tried to commit suicide and had been institutionalized.

SIXTEEN

God forbid that I should go to any heaven
in which there are no horses.

—ROBERT B. CUNNINGHAM

I had the pleasure of meeting Lauren Bacall at an April 2001 trib-
ute to sweet Dudley Moore at Carnegie Hall in New York City.
I've always been an admirer of hers, like everybody else in the
world. But it was her marriage to Humphrey Bogart, twenty-four
years her senior, that naturally has always intrigued me. After the
event, there was a dinner at the Essex House hotel. I hung tight to
Lauren until we were led to our tables. Then I maneuvered my
way into the seat next to her before anyone else could. I told her
how much I had enjoyed reading her autobiography *By Myself*, and
especially how comforting I had found her account of Bogey's
death in 1957 and the fact that she wasn't afraid to reveal the gory
details. Somewhat to my surprise, she told me that it felt good to
write about that period of her life.

*   *   *

In May of 1998, I was in Los Angeles to promote *Wind on Water*, a new TV series that had just been picked up by NBC. With the afternoon free, I went to see the movie *City of Angels* with some friends. John was up at the ranch. While saying goodbye to a visitor, he clutched his chest and said, "I think I'm having a heart attack." Then he collapsed. The visitor helped him into the house, led him to a chair, and called 911.

By the time the fire department got there, John was unconscious and not breathing. Oh, how I wish he had stayed that way, the way it was meant to be. Ironic, really, that he should go that way; whenever we would see someone in a movie grab his chest and drop dead, John would say, "Lucky son of a bitch." But he was revived and taken to the hospital.

City of Angels is about a heart surgeon (played by Meg Ryan) who falls in love with an angel (Nicholas Cage) who collects the souls of patients she loses in the operating room. On the way out of the theater, I never thought that I would be living the movie within a few hours.

The NBC event to promote the series was across the street at the Century City Hotel, where I was staying. I ran to my room, did a quick change, and went with my friends to a big tent at the back of the hotel to watch Diana Ross perform. Three hotel security guards came up to me, handed me a phone, and said I had a call. It was my girlfriend Layla.

"Bo, John is in the hospital. It's serious, and you should get up there right away." She had called our friend Rob Lowe and said, "Rob, something's happened to John. All I know is that Bo is in L.A.; you have to find her!" I still don't know how you found me, but thanks, Rob.

By the time I got to the hospital, one hundred and fifty miles north of L.A., John was in surgery. I had authorized the procedure by cell phone, as the hotel's head of security was racing me up Highway 101. I wish I hadn't okayed it, and I knew when I did that it was the wrong thing to do, but . . . hindsight and all that.

As I came through the hospital doors, I saw that two of our friends were there; I was shocked at how distressed they looked. Brigitta explained that John regained consciousness just before he went in for surgery. She was with him when the surgeon asked John if he wanted surgery. John couldn't speak, so he blinked his eyes twice for yes. The last thing Brigitta told him was "Bo is on her way, and the dogs are okay!" She said that his eyes got big, and he looked happy. Thank you, Brigitta.

Kerry joined me by then; and we all went to a waiting room. I kept thinking about *City of Angels*, and how I had thought while watching the film that the lighting was unattractive. The fluorescent effect was really unflattering for Meg Ryan. Now here I was sitting in the hospital looking around and realizing just how authentic the cold, blue lighting really was in the movie.

After a couple of hours of staring at the walls and heaving big sighs, the surgeon, a very kind young man, appeared in front of us. The operation had gone fairly well, he said; I could see John. I wasn't so shocked by his appearance; actually, he looked quite good, considering he had become combative in the ambulance and had broken his teeth in the ensuing fight. The myriad tubes and hoses didn't bother me much. I was used to seeing them on Russ, my stepson, who was so often in the hospital, near death from complications of paralysis. I looked around at the dozen or so physicians, nurses, and technicians working the pumps, hoses, and other machines, trying so hard to keep him alive. I felt sorry for them, and I was overwhelmed by their dedication and the gentle expressions they gave me when our eyes met. All of a sudden buzzers and sirens on the machines went off, and I was asked to leave the room.

The surgeon came into the waiting room and explained that they were "going back in" to see what had gone wrong. I told him, "If John dies this time . . . please don't bring him back."

He didn't die. Worse, he was on life support. John's coronary arteries had ruptured; all of them, even down into his spleen, like a run in a stocking. I can't really remember exactly, but the surgeon said something about there being some sort of legal technicality about keeping John on life support for twenty-four hours to see if he might regain consciousness. I didn't want him to regain consciousness. But I didn't know how to tell anyone that I had such horrible thoughts, so I agreed.

John would have been furious if he'd come to. This wasn't our deal. He never wanted to be infirm or an invalid. Hell, he didn't want to get old. He wasn't good at it. Bette Davis said, "Getting old is not for sissies." John had, up until this point, been blessed with the miracle waters for which Ponce de León had been searching. At seventy-one, he was uncannily youthful. The skin that he had always baked in the sun (there was an ongoing contest between John and George Hamilton as to who was tanner) was remarkably supple and smooth. His mind was still as sharp as ever, especially when he was angry. I think we've all been surprised at how someone you least expect holds on to life. With no hope, they claw and scrape for the final few days. But I knew in my heart that if nature didn't take John, I would wake up one day to a Hemingway-like ending. He'd leave me a note saying, "Fuck this, I'm leaving!" I know this sounds dramatic, but I do believe this of John.

Sitting in the waiting room, I kept thinking, *What if he survives this? What will I do? How will I explain this to him?* I don't feel bad anymore about having those thoughts. John truly believed in the quality of life, and he lived his fully and in a self-satisfying way. As I said, this was our deal, and I was breaking it.

I went in to see him again. I felt nothing, except that I had betrayed him. *I* was responsible for him being hooked up to all these machines. The nurse was very sweet and held his hand with the three tubes attached. As I just stood there and stared at John's shell, she said, "Talk to him, Bo. He can hear you."

I didn't know what to say. John didn't seem to be there anymore. I looked around the room, wondering if, as in *City of Angels*, an angel might be leading his soul out of the room. John was just gone. A ventilator was breathing for him, making his chest move up and down.

I said something stupid like "How are you?" And went back to the waiting room. Family and friends had started to arrive, while I waited for the twenty-four hours to pass. I went to visit John every hour and say more stupid things to him. I was beginning to think that something was seriously wrong with me. I hadn't cried or sobbed or broken down. Instead, I felt angry, bitter, pissed—disgusted, even, although my body would shake uncontrollably.

There were many friends to call. John's condition had been announced on the evening news. People needed to know what was happening, needed to hear in my voice that there was some hope. I couldn't give them any. I called Ursula in Rome; she was so sad, so upset, and so worried about me. I wanted to tell her, "No need to worry about me, Urs. I didn't know it before, but apparently I'm a cold, uncaring bitch."

I called Sean, John's daughter. They had just reunited after not speaking for seventeen years. She was so distraught that I invited her to take part in the "decisions" that were going to have to be made soon. She was crying. Everyone was crying. My head was screaming, *What the hell is wrong with me?*

Linda called. Why is it that Linda always knows what I'm thinking? Yes, I know she is very spiritual—but I personally don't believe in any of that. In the past, I'm embarrassed to admit that I've even made unkind remarks about her spirituality. She said, "Bo, John is gone."

My dam burst, and I blubbered into the phone, "Linda, the nurse says that I should talk to him, that he can hear me. But I can't think of anything to say to him!"

"Don't worry about any of that," said Linda. "Don't worry about how to act or what to say. He's gone. He's worried about you, but he's in a place where he can't help you."

"I feel so bad that I haven't cried for him until now," I said. "Did you talk to him? Did you see him?"

Linda hesitated. "Yes," she said finally. "And he's okay, but he's in a sort of spiritual limbo. You might be able to talk to him in about six months, if you want to. Or you may not ever want to, and that's okay, too."

"Oh, Linda, it feels so good to cry," I said. "Thank you."

She said, "Bo, you have to take care of yourself now. You can't do anything for John, he's gone. Just take care of you. There are no rules. Do whatever feels right for you."

I went to find the surgeon to order that life support be turned off immediately. It was actually very uneventful when it happened. Sean, Kerry, Layla, and I were there.

He would have liked knowing that he died surrounded by beautiful women.

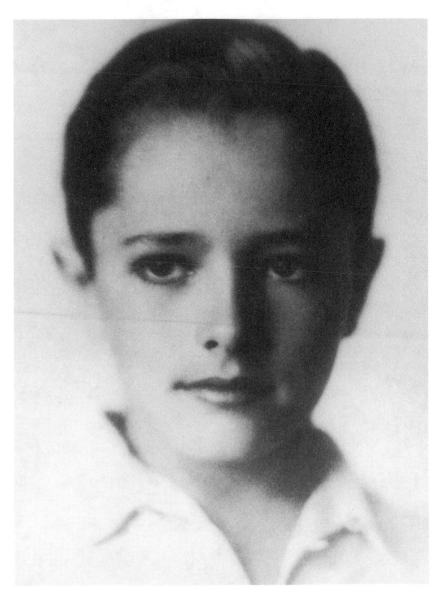

John Derek, 1926–1998

SEVENTEEN

Look, what a horse should have he did not lack,
Save a proud rider on his back.

—WILLIAM SHAKESPEARE

Mares live in harems of two to eight, led by one dominant stallion— an arrangement I think many men would find satisfactory. If the dominant stallion suddenly dies, all the bachelor stallions in the area show up to try to take over the herd. Even long-in-the-tooth, shaggy, lame ones. They will swell up, strut, and try to look their most impressive: laying back their ears, flexing their muzzles, and rolling their eyes. They will fight among one another, often leading to serious injury or death.

But the mares will ultimately decide which stallion will be the leader of the herd. It doesn't matter how strong or dominant a stallion is. It's up to the girls, because there is no rape in the horse world. In fact, when a stallion mounts a mare, he is putting himself at great peril. One stiff kick from the mare and he might limp away with a broken hind leg or an injury that could become infected. Either way, it's sure death for the stallion—an arrangement I think most women would find satisfactory.

Even if the mare is receptive and wants to be bred, Mother Nature still has some dirty tricks to play on the poor guy. When the

217

mare is in heat, her labia becomes very wet, and her tail hairs—which are as strong and coarse as piano strings—tend to get stuck to the entrance of her vulva. As the stallion enters her and makes his first thrust, his penis may be sliced vertically like a sausage.

When a stallion approaches a mare, he uses many senses to read her mood. Chief among them is his highly developed sense of smell. He'll sniff at a mare's face, her breath, all over her body. He'll even spend considerable time sniffing her manure, sniffing for some sign that he can breed her.

A stallion can actually smell when a mare is in heat. He smells the elevated level of estrogen in her urine, and when he gets a whiff of some really choice urine, he *flehmens*. That means he exposes an olfactory zone called Jacobson's organ in the roof of his mouth by raising his neck and head high into the air, then curling his lip back completely. Let me tell you that even the most beautiful, powerful, masculine stallion looks absolutely *ridiculous* when he flehmens: his body all stretched out, his eyes rolled back in his head, his penis hanging down limply, and his upper lip wrinkled and curled back.

Very soon—way too soon—after John died, I started getting calls from some men friends that John and I had known together. At first, they seemed so caring and concerned. One man, the husband of a girlfriend, began calling and talking to me for hours. "How are you doing, Bo?" he would ask. "How are you coping? I'm so concerned about you."

"Oh, I'm okay," I replied.

"Hey, I'm flying in to L.A. for an afternoon meeting on Tuesday," he said. "I'll have the jet stop in Santa Barbara on the way home; we can have dinner and a nice long talk."

"Gee, David, that would be really nice," I said. "I haven't seen you and Suzy in so long."

"Oh, Suzy won't be able to come," he said.

God, I was so gullible. I bragged to my girlfriend Layla about how kind and caring David was. She said, "You idiot, he's sniffing! Has Suzy called you even once?" Because Layla is a horsewoman too, I immediately knew what she meant by sniffing.

"No way," I said. "It's too soon."

Then my memory replayed the many phone conversations with David, and I thought, Oh my God! She's right!

An old friend—and I mean old both in age and in years of friendship—called too. He's a super-rich, wonderful, angry curmudgeon; nearly deaf from his years as a mercenary in various African wars.

"Hi, Bo," he said.

I screamed into the phone as loudly as I could, *"Jim! How are you?"*

He growled, "I'm still alive, barely. I've had three heart attacks, and I'm just waiting for the next one. It'll come any minute. Sorry about John. What about you? Did that son of a bitch leave you with any money?"

"Oh, Jim, you know John, he never worried about things like that," I said. "But I'll be all right. What about you? Are you in love again?"

"Nah," he replied. "Are you available?"

He was deadly serious. "Jim!" I laughed. "Give me a little time!"

But as one of my girlfriends Robin pointed out, "Bo, you've got to give him credit for throwing his hat into the ring."

Less obvious was a man I've known since I was sixteen. He was also an old friend of John's and knew both of us separately before John and I met. I just can't use his name, for he is very well known. He walks with such a distinctive toes-splayed-out-to-the-side walk that my girlfriend Nancy calls him "Walks Like a Duck." There have always been rumors that Walks Like a Duck is bisexual, so his friendship with John always made me—and certainly John—a little uncomfortable.

Nonetheless, I thought of Walks Like a Duck as a good pal of twenty-six years. I'd known him since the days when we were all struggling and poor, then through our respective successes, when I became *Bo*, and he became a movie mogul. Over the years, he always said, "Bo, if anything ever happens to John, I will take care of you. Never worry about anything."

About ten days after John's death, Walks Like a Duck roared up to the ranch in his hot-red Ferrari like some knight in shining armor. He was wearing skintight bicycle pants that showed off a respectable bulge between his legs.

"I wanted to see how you're doing and to help you with things," he said in greeting. "I want you to know that I'm here for you."

I told him the truth. Financial ups and downs have always been a part of my life. I've been richer than I ever dreamed possible and down to my last fifty dollars so many times that I've never been embarrassed about it.

"Well, I do have some real financial problems and would be grateful for any help," I told Walks Like a Duck. I explained that my debt was less than the appraised value of the ranch, so I was covered there. "But I've got this TV series in Hawaii that I start next month," I added. "So I won't be here to sell the ranch myself."

Walks Like a Duck said that he was extremely concerned about my emotional state and said that I shouldn't have to think about such stressful matters as selling the ranch. He bragged about his talents in real estate and said that he would take care of everything for me. *What a break!* I thought. I was so relieved.

We went to lunch with my sister Kerry at my favorite taco joint. It wasn't compatible with Duck's Zone diet, so he didn't eat much. He seemed restless and distracted. I thought it was because he was concerned about me and that he was trying to read me. Otherwise, why would he keep making such serious eye contact, staring deeply into my eyes and repeating assurances that he would always be "there" for me?

Kerry was sitting on the other side of Walks Like a Duck. She kicked me under the table, slyly nodded in his direction, and started sniffing and rubbing a finger under her nose. I thought, *Kerry, why don't you go get a Kleenex or something?*

Finally, it hit me: *Oh, shit! She's telling me that he's sniffing.* I kicked her back to knock it off. At first I thought it was absurd. Walks wouldn't do that. He's one of my oldest and dearest friends. When we got back to the ranch, we sat out in the courtyard next to the lap pool that John had built for me because I love to swim. Walks Like a Duck got down to business. First, he said that he needed to know the exact details of my debt. Kerry got some pencils and legal pads, and we did the math.

"Okay," I said finally. "My mortgage is about $1.9 million. I owe the IRS about $300,000 in back taxes and a little more on credit cards—actually, five different credit cards."

"No problem," said Walks Like a Duck. "I'll just buy the ranch from you. Then you won't have to worry about a thing. You may not know it, but this is a very rough time for you. Go off to Hawaii and try to have fun."

Wow, I thought. *What a relief!* Just like that, my money troubles were over! I kicked Kerry under the table and stuck my tongue out at her when he wasn't looking. Shame on her for thinking he wasn't a true friend.

"Let's see," said my savior, starting to crunch the numbers. "I'll give you $1,900,000 for the ranch, so that you will be out of your mortgage. I can even get this all finished before you leave."

The ranch had been appraised for $2,800,000. Walks Like a Duck was a cool million short.

BO DEREK

"But what about the rest of my debt?" I said. "You're almost a million short of the appraised value! And that doesn't even touch what I owe the IRS."

He stared me right in the eyes, absolutely caring and sincere.

"Bo, take my advice, you're in no state to deal with all this," he said.

"But—"

"Trust me, the best thing you can do right now is get out of your mortgage. Then you can work out a deal to pay off the rest of your debt over time," he said.

Kerry gave me another big kick under the table. It wasn't necessary. I understood *exactly* what was going on.

I thanked him for his generosity and said that I would fax the papers right away. I never did, and he never called.

Kerry and Nancy and I don't call him Walks Like a Duck anymore. We call him "Shithead."

I could try to make the case that all of the men who came around sniffing were like stallions, all following some very primitive instinct, something essential to the survival of the species. But these guys? I think they'd just heard all those stories about widows submerging their pain and grief in wild sex. They were just trying to get laid.

In August I went off to Hawaii to work on *Wind on Water*. What a blessing to have to go to work at such a time—and in paradise, no less. The big island of Hawaii is a magical, mystical place, and it was good for me to be alone and to experience my first few months as a widow in such a beautiful setting.

Back home, I had to face the first major decision of my new life without John: selling the ranch. I had asked Kerry to put it on the market while I was working. I was making good money on the series; plenty to keep the ranch going, but I wanted to be debt-free in my new life. Television is famous for its unpredictability, and I didn't want to throw all my money into my mortgage. I no longer wanted the responsibility of forty-five acres of ranch and seven thousand square feet of house, and other buildings that needed constant attention and care. When you have a partner, these things are joys. When you are alone, they are burdens. I had already sold most of my twenty-six horses, which made the whole process much easier.

Kerry put the ranch up for sale. She would report to me about the different showings and expressions of interest. One day she called and said that a star of a major prime-time television series and his then fiancée had come to see the ranch. I didn't know them. But Kerry said that they were a wonderful couple who seemed to really understand the place. They had spent most of the day going over every detail. Kerry had even taken over the showing from the Realtor because the couple seemed to love the stories she told about some of the ranch's unusual features.

"Bo, you'll love them, and you will want them to have it," she said.

I really didn't care about the ranch as much as everyone thought I did. Yes, I absolutely loved my life there. Those are memories that I will keep forever. But they are not tied to the land or any place on a map. I carry my happy times in my heart and my mind.

The TV star and his fiancée kept coming to see the ranch. One day Kerry called me in Hawaii. "They want to come up on Sunday and have a picnic," she said. "I have to take P. J. [Kerry's son] to a judo tournament, and I won't be here. The real-estate agent says, 'Absolutely not. Don't let them visit the house alone.' What do you want me to do?"

"Oh, let them come," I said without hesitation. "I don't care. Let them enjoy it. Ask the housekeeper to be there but to leave them alone."

I didn't think it would make them want to buy the ranch more. In fact, so much time had passed since they first looked at it, we had pretty much decided that they weren't going to buy it. But what the hell, I thought. Let them have a good time.

Monday morning Kerry called and said that the picnic had done the trick; the actor had made an offer. She also said that they had taken all my dogs out to a far hill and spent the day there. That I didn't like. I know it's petty, but I'm very covetous of my dogs' affections.

I was asking $2,850,000, the bank-appraised value of the ranch. The offer was for $2,300,000.

I countered with $2,750,000. The housing market was picking up, so I didn't have to give the ranch away. He came back at $2,400,000, and I said, "No, thank you." Well, everyone went nuts. The agents said that I couldn't just say no; I had to counter. "No, I don't!" I said. That was that, in my mind.

My TV series was not going well. One Monday morning, after completing our eighth episode, I called a producer about some problems I had with the new script. He seemed distracted, not paying attention to anything I was saying.

"What is it?" I finally asked.

"Oh, nothing, Bo," he said.

But I knew. Instantly. "They've canceled the show, haven't they?" I said.

"I think so," he replied glumly. "The head of the studio was just fired, and I think we're going with him."

I called the local production office, and the secretary confirmed that today would be the last day of shooting. Just like that. "When would you like to go home?" she asked.

There is something so refreshing about moving on. And I like departures to be swift and clean. "The next plane out," I said.

"Oh, Bo, you don't have to leave so fast," she said. "Take your time. You've been here for three months. Isn't it going to take you some time to pack?"

"The next plane leaves in three hours. Please book me on it," I said.

I wasn't angry or even sad that *Wind on Water* was canceled. The network had to do what it had to do. I was grateful for the experience. But I was also getting tired of fighting for script changes and suffering from a bit of island fever. And, frankly, I was beginning to doubt my ability to judge the writing. Maybe the changes I wanted were making the stories worse.

I made it back home on Tuesday. It was so good to see the dogs and the horses and the views that I loved so much. But being back in the house was not especially meaningful for me. I was plenty tired, but I saw no reason to possibly think about *it* all night, so I took a sleeping pill and went to bed.

At about 4:00 A.M. I bolted upright, wide awake. *I've got to get out now!* I said to myself. *If I don't, it will start all over again.*

It was the debt. I was haunted by it.

The next morning I went into the kitchen. Kerry was cooking my nephew P. J. and my niece MacKenzie breakfast. "Call the real-estate agents," I said. "Tell them to tell the buyer that if he wants the ranch, I'll sell it for $2.5 million. But no contingencies and the fastest escrow possible. The offer is good only until the end of the day. That will leave me with $100,000 in my pocket, and it will all be over by Christmas."

Kerry looked shocked. "You should get more, and two other buyers are interested," she said. But she understood my feelings and got on it right away.

It took the actor only a few hours to accept the offer. What a relief! I felt good that the ranch was going to a young couple in love. *Maybe things are going to be all right after all*, I thought, feeling quite clever at the way I had taken charge.

Escrow would close on December 18, 1998. A few days later, the actor's business manager asked whether he could send over a house inspector. But our agreement was for no contingencies, and that included an inspection.

"Not part of the deal," I said.

"Oh, it's only for his personal use," the manager replied. "There is some remodeling he would like to do, and this will help him budget it."

My lawyer said I shouldn't allow it, but I thought, *Why not?* If the roles were reversed, I would appreciate the seller letting me inspect the house. Besides, I had nothing to hide.

Everything seemed to be going along swimmingly. My entire extended family, all twenty-two of us, had a wonderful final Thanksgiving at the ranch. To top it off, a new friend, Peter, called on that very day of giving thanks and generously offered me and my immediate family—which consisted of Kerry, her family, my dogs, my horses, and my parrot—a lovely house in a vineyard to live in until I "got organized." Because until the phone rang, I had no idea where I'd be moving in three weeks.

Then on December 7—Pearl Harbor Day—disaster struck. We were in the middle of trying to move twenty years' worth of accumulated stuff. My days were spent trying to decide what to keep for my new solo life, what to give away, what to chuck, what to store. A letter arrived from the actor's business manager saying that the inspection had revealed some shocking safety issues with the ranch. The letter stated that the remodeling we had performed over the years had been done in a less than standard and safe manner, and not to code.

Among the many claims: In the event of an earthquake of a certain seismic magnitude, the roof could become detached, causing catastrophic failure to the entire house. (*No shit!* That's what earthquakes do!) The old electrical wiring could burn down the whole place. The fireplaces posed serious fire hazards. And on and on. The bottom line? The acctor wanted to reduce the price by $150,000.

The letter ended with: "We regret having to burden Ms. Derek with this request at this sensitive time, realizing that selling her home is stressful on its own." At least they were right about that. Kerry and I went into a panic. The movers were coming in four days.

I called Tony, our longtime friend and contractor, and asked him what was going on. He told me to calm down, assuring me that everything had been built to code. "In fact," he said, "John usually insisted that it be built above code. All the permits will be on file with the county."

As Kerry drove over to the courthouse to collect all the permits, I began my education in Santa Barbara County building codes and engineering. Having lived in the valley for eighteen years, I knew I had many friends there. But I had no idea how a community could come together to help one of their own. Tony got the word out—"Bo's being screwed!"—and within days workmen began arriving at the ranch to make inspections and give me written reports. There was John, the structural engineer; Lonnie, the electrician; Mark, the plumber; Mark, the carpenter; Jerry, the termite inspector; Johnny, the fireplace inspector; Jesus, the gardener; Brad, the handyman; and Tom, the grader.

I was overwhelmed at how they came to my rescue and the love that came from these old friends. They absolutely refused to be paid for their time. "We're just happy to help you out," they said. "And don't worry, Bo, we'll never work for the new owner."

"No, please *do* work for him," I said. "Just charge him triple!"

I sent the stack of reports and permits and a letter declining to change the selling price. I knew that the house was sound inside and out—and I think they knew it, too. To my mind, it was all a ruse to force down the price.

Kerry and I were emotional wrecks. I drank too much red wine for me, two glasses every night. I'd never really believed that stress could affect your health in a dramatic way, but that November and December I had the you-want-to-die flu, a yeast infection, a hemorrhagic bladder infection, a sinus infection, and migraines. I also thought I needed a root canal, but it turned out that I was grinding my teeth in my sleep, which was totally dependent on sleeping pills.

My friend Lady Romney said, "Darling, you're looking terrible."

She was right. I was getting thin, my hair was dull, my skin was gray, and I just didn't give a damn. The house was a maze of boxes. The movers were on day-to-day standby. Everything I owned was packed up, ready to go nowhere.

Finally, the actor's business manager called.

"We know Bo's financial situation," the business manager told the real-estate agent. "We know her debts. We also know that she has to sell the ranch by the end of the fiscal year of her husband's death, or else she will have to pay a fortune in taxes. My client wants some money back, or we will just wait until after the first of the year. Then we can start this whole process over again."

Kerry began ranting and raving. Funny, all I felt was an incredible sense of calm and peace. I felt as though I had won a great victory. No one could say that I had tried to sell a lame house.

My lawyer was furious and said that I had to fight this to the end. Kerry agreed. "Don't give in," she said. "It's better to lose the ranch to the bank. That's what John would do."

The real-estate agents were embarrassed. Even the actor's real-estate agent called to apologize. I was reminded of the old serial films with the widow tied to the train tracks and villainous Dastardly Dan twirling his mustache while a train barrels toward her.

I figured that if they wanted $150,000 I was supposed to counter with half. So I offered $75,000. It was Friday, and the business manager was so relieved. "This is wonderful news!" he exclaimed. "My client will be so happy. He loves the house so much. Merry

Christmas!" He added that the buyer was away for the weekend but that he would be able to reach him.

We called the movers and began moving again.

Then, first thing Monday, the business manager called. His tone had changed. He said that he was very sorry if he had given us the impression that $75,000 would be enough. He had spoken to his client, and he wanted a $100,000 reduction.

"Is that all?" I asked sarcastically. "Are you sure he doesn't want any more?"

My girlfriend Rona said that I shouldn't pay another penny. She suggested that the real-estate agents pay the $25,000 difference. Kerry called them, and they instantly agreed. My cynical side felt that the agents agreed because they were afraid of losing a huge commission, but I also believed them when they said that they were embarrassed by what had happened.

Whenever I tell this story, almost everyone tells me, "Bo, I'm sure the buyer had no idea what happened. His business manager must be a real bastard. He has the reputation of being the nicest guy. He would never do that to you."

I'm sorry, but I've had bastard business managers too. I strongly doubt that the business manager came to him and said, "That Bo, she's such a nice girl! She just had this incredible urge to give you $100,000 back from the sale of your new home. Whatta gal!"

Oh, well, it's long since over. I sold the ranch. I'm glad he bought it. And I'm grateful that he bought before the end of the year. He enabled me to move on with my life, which in the end was more important than the $100,000 I was hoping to come away with.

EIGHTEEN

It's best not to swap horses while crossing a river.

—ABRAHAM LINCOLN

One of the benefits of writing a book about your life is to set the record straight. So let me take this opportunity to say that there has never been anything between Ted Turner and me. I have met him only twice in my whole life, and nothing—absolutely nothing—happened. But sometimes the truth is even more compelling than the rumors.

The first time I met Ted was in December 1981 while scouting location for a pirate film that never got made. John and I landed at the Athens airport to catch a plane to Rome, where we were going to visit Ursula. I saw Ted Turner walk by with a pretty blonde.

I knew of Ted Turner because I had grown up in a family that sailed. Ted had won the ultimate sailing race, the America's Cup, in 1977. Between that and his colorful personality, he became something of a hero around our home.

"That's Ted Turner," I said to John.

"Who's Ted Turner?" he replied.

I explained: great sailor, real character, and starting a cable news channel to be called Cable News Network. John knew about CNN and was interested in it because he believed that it would be good to have an alternative to the three major networks. And he certainly admired anyone who would try to buck the establishment.

"That couldn't be Ted Turner," John said, watching the couple. "He would have an entourage."

"Look at us," I said. "We don't have an entourage."

John dismissed what I'd said, sure that I was wrong. As we waited to board, Ted walked by us a few times and kept glancing over. I could tell he recognized us. Finally he came over and introduced himself and his pretty blonde companion. Her name was Liz Wickersham. Ted said that he was traveling the world to set up affiliate stations for his fledgling cable network, which was about six months away from debuting. When we mentioned that we were on our way to see Ursula Andress, he was very interested. Somehow it was arranged that he and Liz would join us that night for dinner with Urs.

Our flight started to board. As the first-class passengers started to form a line, Ted went to the other line. John asked, "What the hell are you doing over there?" Ted explained that he was asking everyone in his network to fly tourist—a radical idea to the three major networks at the time—so he felt he had to set the example.

John always had a big problem traveling. He hated everything about it: standing in line, being told where to go and what time to go there, where to sit, and generally being treated like cattle. John was from a time when travel was exclusive and civilized. Just as we had begun this trip around the world, the first hijacking of a passenger jet had occurred, and security searches and frisking had begun at some airports.

John couldn't handle being frisked. He couldn't even handle being asked to take off his coat for no good reason. There weren't handheld metal detectors back then, so the boys would have to go in one line and the girls in another to be patted down. Whenever I got through my line, I would look over to where John was supposed to come out. More often than not, I would see him being led away by the police. He always had a very smug look on his face and would say to me, "Don't worry, just don't get on the plane, no matter what. If I'm not back in an hour, go to the embassy."

One thing that John always relied on was that when he was taken to headquarters, the chief would usually be about his own age and would recognize him. They would invariably begin talking about Hollywood. In the end, the chief would ask for John's autograph and let him go with nothing more than a "Bon voyage!"

Okay, back to Ted. That afternoon in Rome, Ted called and said that he wanted to come to our hotel about a half hour early because there was something he wanted to talk to us about. We couldn't imagine what it could be.

Ted arrived with Liz, and he was terribly serious. He explained that he had just made a deal with evangelist Jerry Falwell and his recently founded Moral Majority. At the time, the conservative political action group was all over the news and seemed to us to be a real threat to free speech. Ted explained that making this deal was the only way he could get the affiliate stations he needed throughout the largely conservative Midwest. He went on to explain that he had had to make associations to get the network going. We weren't sure why Ted felt compelled to tell us this, but he said that he wanted us to hear it from him before it came out in the news.

Off we went to dinner. Ted was obviously smitten with Ursula, and it must have been very funny for Ted to be there with John and me. Liz Wickersham was smart and fun, and we all had a great time.

That was the last time I saw Ted until February 1999, twenty years later. I attended a dinner for the Nuclear Age Peace Foundation. My friends Gerry Spence, the famed trial attorney, and his wife, Imaging, are on the board, and they asked me to be their guest. My girlfriend Diandra Douglas was also hosting it. She's a fellow horse breeder with whom I have gone riding in Spain and Portugal. I knew that Ted Turner was to be honored that night.

Ted gave a terrific speech when he accepted his award, and wife Jane Fonda was there with him. I had heard that they were having marital problems, but I never give credence to those kinds of rumors. During the event, Ted starting walking around the room. As he walked by, I said hello and introduced myself. I remained seated; he was standing. We never even shook hands. He immediately reminded me of the time we met in Athens and had dinner in Rome with Ursula. I was surprised that he recalled the details of that chance encounter so long ago. I wouldn't have imagined that it was such an unusual night for him.

That was it; that was all that happened. A few days later it was reported in the tabloids that Ted and I were having an affair and that during dinner we had snuck off to the bushes for a quickie! It was so ridiculous I found it funny; but it was an early sign of what my life was going to be like now that I was single. The story made its way out of the tabloids and into the mainstream press all over the world. Urs called from Rome, screaming, "What is this with Ted Turner?"

Another friend called, saying, "You and Ted are perfect for each other! He likes the same things you do—the sea, horses, ranches—and he's rich!"

People were so truly happy for me. Ted was rich, so *I* was going to be rich. Everything was going to be glorious. Many of my friends were sincerely disappointed when I told them that the rumors weren't true. I think some of them believed that there must have been some fire to this smoke. I'll never convince them otherwise.

That first year of widowhood brought many reports about my love affairs, including Paul McCartney, whom I have never met; and Keifer Sutherland, whom I think I did meet once at a team penning; and his Serene Highness Prince Albert of Monaco. I did have dinner with him once. But most incessant were the Ted Turner rumors; they popped up about every three months. One day the editor of a newspaper called me about my dinner with Ted the night before at the

Polo Lounge in the Beverly Hills Hotel. According to his "sources," I was dressed in casual white and the two of us were holding hands across the table. I said, "Oh, that sounds so wonderful! Print it!" But in the end I had to confess that I had spent the night alone in bed with my two German shepherds. This admission led to a new series of headlines: CELIBATE BO!

Just before Easter 2000 the Ted Turner story hit again, and it hit hard. It was on every national news channel. Fox News and even CNN reported it every hour for the entire day. They would show lovely clips of me riding my horses, then show Ted riding *his* horses. I was sailing, then he was sailing. By now, Ted and Jane were officially separated, which no doubt helped fuel the story.

It was a wild week. The phone never stopped ringing. Urs even called again to joke about it. A duchess friend called from Spain to pass along an offer from a magazine of at least one hundred thousand dollars for the "exclusive" story, and she said I could probably get more. Oh, I was tempted. Maybe Ted wouldn't mind. I was broke, the story was already being printed, what could it hurt? I enjoyed thinking about it and even fantasized about making up a wild story. But in the end, I just couldn't.

About a week later, I got a call from my agent asking if he could give my home number to a very well-respected publicist who wanted to talk to me about something personal. "Sure," I said. At the same time, my really good girlfriend Rona Barrett called on the other line to ask if she could give my home number to this same publicist. "Sure," I said. But it made me feel a little uneasy that someone should need to speak to me so urgently.

About five minutes later, the publicist called.

"Jane Fonda wants to talk to you about something personal," she said, adding, "but don't worry."

I thought, *What does she mean, "don't worry?"* Now I *was* worried.

"Of course, give her my number," I said.

Five minutes later, Jane called. I was a bit nervous. After our greetings, I told Jane that I wanted her to know that I had absolutely nothing to do with all the rumors swirling around.

"Well, that's sort of why I'm calling," she said. "Bo, are you ready to start seeing someone?"

"Funny enough, it's been a year and a half since John died, and I *have* been thinking about it," I said.

Jane said that she wanted me to know that she and Ted were officially separated. Although she was crazy about him and still loved him, they were not going to get back together.

I think I said, "Oh."

She went on to say that she and Ted had dined together the night before to discuss a possible reconciliation, but they both decided that it wasn't going to work.

I probably said, "Oh."

She said that she had asked Ted about the rumors about me and if there was anything to them. I was then completely confused and had no idea where this conversation was headed. Actually that's not true. I had a pretty good idea, but I couldn't bring myself to believe it. My pulse was quickening.

Recounting their conversation, Jane said that Ted had told her that there was nothing to the rumors, "So I told him, 'Ted, you should think about Bo. I don't know her personally, but she was deeply in love with her husband. She loves the outdoors and horses, and I have heard that she is a good person. Why shouldn't you meet her? She could be perfect for you.' "

By now I was on the floor writhing. I couldn't believe what I was hearing and that I was hearing it from *Jane Fonda*. And she was talking about *Ted Turner*, her husband! My face turned beet red, and I broke out in a sweat. Kerry was watching me, totally confused by my behavior.

I cut Jane off midsentence. "Jane, when I said before that I was thinking that maybe I am ready to start seeing someone, I didn't mean anything like this. This is too weird."

"Why?"

"Because it's you, and it's him, and you're his wife, and I'm not ready for this!"

She told me that she loved Ted and just wanted him to be happy. She described him as the most wonderful, generous, fun, intelligent man. She said that he was sixty-one years old, but in good health. And that while he suffered from a bad back, he was a great lover.

"Stop! I don't want to know all this!" Jane Fonda was giving me Ted Turner's vet check. *So* much more information than I wanted.

When you buy a horse, you have a veterinarian check the horse from head to toe; similar to our own annual physical. You don't want to buy a pig in a poke, so the vet will also have the horse walk and trot, looking for signs of lameness. If you are buying a breeding stallion, the vet will also check sperm count and motility.

"Jane, I really can't deal with this right now," I said, then tried to lighten the tone of the conversation. "I thought that I had married into a weird relationship with John and Ursula and Linda. But this is too much. This is too bizarre."

Again: "Why?" She was so serious.

"Because you're his wife."

Jane was not deterred at all. She said Ted would be in L.A. in a couple of weeks because they had originally planned to see a counselor there about their marriage. Although they had decided not to see the counselor, Ted would still be coming. "You two can have dinner," she said. By then, I was back on the floor, mouthing *"Fuck! This is too weird!"* to Kerry.

"Bo, you have to understand that although Ted is a powerful man, in a situation like this he would never be able to call you himself, for fear of rejection," Jane said. "That's why I am calling." She went on to explain that he had 1.7 million acres of ranch land, had done so much for the environment, and had introduced bison back onto one of his ranches. "Bo, you would love his ranch in New Mexico!" she said. "You love horses, and you will love his quarter horses and his breeding program for them."

Now I was beginning to allow myself to be lulled by this truly great saleswoman.

"So will you have dinner with Ted?" she persisted.

I almost said yes. Then caught myself and said that I wanted to think about it over the Easter weekend. Jane said okay and asked me to call her Monday morning.

"Sure I will."

Kerry and I had decided that we should not tell anyone. Well, except for Mom, of course, and my friend Layla and . . . within hours I had told every one of my girlfriends. I think if this had happened to me now, I would be all right with it. But back then, at that time in my life, it was one of the most outrageous things I had ever experienced. Kerry and I would look at each other and just burst out laughing.

Layla remarked, "Bo, it doesn't get any better than this." Another made me promise to bring her to the ranch in New Mexico. Most were just happy for me because Ted was so rich. Ursula thought it was hilarious and wanted to know if Jane would be coming to dinner. I had this strange feeling that I was the victim of some elaborate practical joke. *Blake Edwards must be behind this somehow*, I thought. But it sure sounded like Jane on the phone, and my agent and Rona Barrett would have known if it had not really been the publicist calling. They wouldn't take part in this joke, would they?

By Monday morning, I had decided to go to dinner with Ted. Why not? At 9:00 sharp, after I'd finished feeding the horses and dogs and, finally, myself—the animals come first—the phone rang.

"It's Jane Fonda," said Kerry. Wasn't I supposed to call her?

"Yeah, sure," I said, taking the phone, thinking that it must be my mother, who was, by then, in on all the latest. But it wasn't. It was Jane. "So, what do you think?" she asked. "Will you have dinner with Ted?"

"Jane," I said, "Ted and I must have a thousand people we know through a friend of a friend that could have made this call for him. But the fact that you've called, well, I'm having a big problem with it."

She said, "Why?"

"Because you're his wife," I repeated. "But I'm feeling adventurous. So, yes, of course I will have dinner with Ted."

Jane sounded very happy. She reiterated how much I would like him, how wonderful and generous Ted was, and, oh, yes: "He knows he has to be faithful now."

Jane said, "There is only one problem."

"Oh? What?"

"Ted could never be with a woman who has a career in movies."

"Well, I only have a career to support my horse habit," I said as a joke, then paused. "But wait a minute! We're just going to have dinner. You're talking long-term!"

"With Ted, you'll never have to work again," Jane said.

I think I mouthed *Fuck! Fuck! Fuck!*" to Kerry. I don't normally swear like this. Well, only in extreme circumstances. And, this was extreme.

She asked if this was the right phone number for Ted to call. I said yes.

She said, "Where could you two go that would be discrete? I guess you and Ted can work that out when he calls."

I said I thought that was a good idea.

I spent the next two weeks dying, wondering how I would handle the next part of this drama.

Guess what? Ted never called.

NINETEEN

Some glory in their birth
Some in their wealth,
Some in their body force
Some in their hounds and hawks,
Some in their horse.

—WILLIAM SHAKESPEARE

It's now been years since I sold the ranch. I still have horses. I still have Centauro and Celosa, although they're getting old. I have a clever little white donkey named Machito. He was a companion for Mouro, but Mouro is gone. So Machito now keeps Celosa company. Cifi, my protector and companion through the rough years, died this year.

I have lost so many pets and friends and bits and pieces of my life. I do have a new mare, Gaiata. The name means "pretty country girl" in Portuguese. She was a gift from a Portuguese breeder. In an ironic way, Gaiata represents a new part of my life. First, she's a mare. I've never ridden a mare before. I mean, yes, I've ridden mares, but this is the first time I have a mare as my riding horse. Before I always rode stallions—difficult, hot-tempered, exciting but dangerous stallions.

Stallions are so preoccupied with breeding that it takes great skill to keep their attention. When riding a stallion, you must always anticipate potential threats to their territory, or what female might attract them. If you don't, you'll find yourself riding around on a stallion with a giant erection.

Gaiata is *so-ooo* different. She's teaching me to be a better, more sensitive, and consistent rider. Once you get a stallion focused on you and what you want, he's very forgiving and, in general, eager to please. Not so with a mare like Gaiata. First, she went into a deep depression when she arrived from Portugal. I'd never seen anything like it in all my years of shipping horses all over the world.

Great! I thought. *I have a sour bitch on my hands.* She would pin her ears back and turn her rump to me whenever I approached her. After a three-month courtship, with me falling all over myself to please her, she started to warm up to me, and we have spent some serious time bonding. Still, in riding, I have to earn every little step she makes for me. She is the most brilliant athlete I have ever ridden. For good reason, she was European Champion of Working Equitation before she was presented to me.

Just as I have been learning more about the equine fair sex, I've also been discovering a feminine side of myself. I actually have girl-friends! Of course, I had female friends when I was with John, but it was different. I was always part of a pair and not very good at having a female friend separate from my husband. Our friends were *our* friends, and we had great friends. But now, even my friendship with the wife of a couple we had as great friends has evolved to a new level of *girlfriend*. It's wonderful: more intimate, secret, sisterly, and fun!

Most of my girlfriends are horsey girls, like I am. *Amazonas.* That's what they call us in Spain and Portugal. I go there three times a year with a new batch of beautiful girlfriends to share my secret world of Iberian horses, fighting bulls, handsome horsemen, and good friends. One year, I brought actress Diandra Douglas, actress Daryl Hannah, Princess Shehkar Jah of India, supermodel Tatiana

Patitz, and Shania Twain. Headlines in newspapers screamed, SEVILLE INVADED BY THE AMAZONAS. The Spanish, who love celebrity and royalty more than anyone, went wild. Between being hounded by the paparazzi, we got in some great rides and spent some dreamy days at some beautiful ranches. Considering we were six girls going without sleep for four days, we got along pretty well. I learned on the first day, however, that I shouldn't be the one to choose who rides which horse. There is always one horse more beautiful than the others, and that's the one everyone wants.

Funny, I consider all of these amazonas good friends, but I couldn't tell you a thing about their personal lives. However, I could go on and on about the bloodlines of their horses, how they ride, and what type of horse pleases them. I had known Daryl Hannah for two years. We had traveled to Spain together twice; we were even semi-related when her mare gave birth to a foal sired by my stallion. One day she called and asked if she could come up to the ranch with her boyfriend. I must have been the only person in the world who didn't know that she had been dating John F. Kennedy, Jr., for three years.

Princess Shehkar and I have ridden together in so many beautiful places and ridden so long and hard, abusing our bodies until we were a mass of sore muscles, bruises, and blisters. Not to mention the special blisters in private places, which cause us to let out blood curdling screams when we pee! My sisters and I make the annual pilgrimage to the Kentucky Derby, where we meet up with friends and trainers and grooms and jockeys. Jockeys are my absolute heroes. Pound for pound, they are undoubtedly the strongest and, by far, the most courageous athletes in all the world.

My interest in horses, combined with my celebrity, has given me the opportunity to travel and make friends all over the world. So much of my life now is a wonderful odyssey, full of invitations to horse shows, horse races; the sport of kings, in exotic places like the

Middle East, South America, and the Orient, where I meet the wealthy, royalty, and world leaders, all of whom share the common interest of horses.

Not everything that gives me pleasure or rings my bell is horse related. But usually sports of some kind are involved. I still love to go to the fights. And my friendship with many great champions gives me much joy. I blush with pride when Muhammad Ali gives me a big smile and asks me, out of a whole room full of people, to sit next to him.

This year, I had the honor to be asked by the Secretary of Veterans Affairs to be national honorary chairperson for the Disabled Veterans special events.

I recently attended the National Disabled Veterans Winter Sports Clinic, as well as the National Veterans Wheelchair Games. What a blast! Imagine hitting a home run with only one hand on the bat—because the other arm is holding your paralyzed torso into your chair. The finals of wheelchair basketball were just as exciting as a Los Angeles Lakers game and much faster. Wheelchair basketball is beautifully graceful. About every fifteen minutes, the strangest odor would fill the auditorium. "Sandy, what's that smell?" I asked. Sandy is a new friend who's dedicated his life to introducing sports to veterans with disabilities.

"Bo, it's burning flesh," he said.

"What?"

"Yeah, they get going so fast that the wheels rub against an arm or a leg, and it burns."

"That's horrible!"

"No it isn't," he said. "Look, they're loving it. Wait until you see quad rugby tonight. If it were dogs playing, it would be outlawed as cruelty to animals." Sandy was right about that. Quad rugby must be the most frightening, intense, sporting event that I've ever seen. Quadriplegics are strapped with duct tape into special wheelchairs that have been modified with wild, *Mad Max*–looking armor plating welded to the fronts and sides—the better for bashing and ramming opponents. The first time I saw a quadriplegic person fly out of his chair, and his head strike the floor, I thought my heart would stop beating right then and there. But sure enough, the player pulled himself up and, with some help from an official, got back in the chair to finish the game with astonishing aggression. Another player was in a chair with a back that was a little too short for the level of his injury. As a result, whenever he got caught off balance, he ended up bent way too far backward over his chair than a human body should. The officials wouldn't let any of the spectators assist him, so he remained helplessly suspended, like a contortionist from Cirque du Soleil, until an official hastened over to put him right again.

I realized that just because these men are disabled, it doesn't mean that they don't have all the testosterone flowing through their veins and have the same urge to bash and hit and take part in contact sports as any other man. They're such superb, talented competitors. And it's not just because they've overcome the obstacles associated with their disabilities, which, having witnessed firsthand from John's late son, Russ, takes a courage I don't think I have. They're just brilliant athletes with more determination and perseverance than I have ever seen.

To see a triple amputee getting air as he comes flying over a rise, downhill skiing, or watching a tenacious paralyzed woman outdo all the men in slalom—these are the most life-affirming sights!

I shed some of my bimbo image during the 2000 presidential campaign.

It was purely accidental. I didn't set out prove myself intelligent; I simply volunteered to help with the election of George W. Bush. Now, I realize that expectations regarding my intellect were low. But people must have really thought I was a total idiot, because after appearing on a few political news shows to explain why I supported Bush, I was suddenly hailed smart by the really smart.

My support was based on his record as governor of Texas. There was also something about how people who knew him—people I respected—raved about him. A contributing factor was my admiration for his parents.

I had met President George Herbert Walker Bush, the forty-first president, several times over the years. The first time was in the White House Oval Office in August 1990. Iraq's Saddam Hussein had just invaded Kuwait, and America was preparing for what would become the Gulf War.

John and I were in D.C. for the Washington International Horse Show, where a friend and fellow Spanish horse breeder had invited me to ride Mouro in a special exhibition. My friend was also showing us the city, which included tours of the Capitol and the White House. During our tour of the Capitol, I ran into a journalist, who asked me the name of my congressman. I was mortified that I didn't know! My brain did a quick review of the signs and banners that I had seen around Santa Ynez (I have something of a photographic memory) and came up with the name Lagomarsino. I didn't know if he was a congressman or a senator but figured I had a fifty-fifty chance. I took a deep big breath and said, "Lagomarsino." Ha! The journalist smiled, wrote something in his notepad, and asked if I was satisfied with Congressman Lagomarsino. "Yes," I said, praying he wasn't a nut. (For the record, Republican Robert J. Lagomarsino is a terrific man and was a well-respected U.S. representative from California for nearly twenty years.) The journalist smiled again and walked off. I vowed then and there to never get caught being so ignorant about something so important again.

Thank God he didn't ask if I was a Democrat or a Republican, because I really wasn't sure. My family had been Democrats. John wasn't, because he couldn't be part of *any* group, just on principle, but he was certainly liberal. All our friends in the film industry were Democrats, especially the odd writers and artist friends of John's. But I wasn't so sure anymore.

The next day we had a private tour of the White House, during which our guide excused himself as he was called to a phone. He returned and said that we had been invited to the West Wing. We followed him there and stood in the waiting room for what seemed like an eternity. We were finally greeted by Andrew Card, then deputy chief of staff, who led us down a hallway. A door opened, and National Security Advisor Brent Scowcroft gave us a great big hello. We turned a corner, yet another door opened, and Chief of Staff John Sununu came out and escorted us into the Oval Office and introduced us to President Bush.

The President invited me to sit in one of *the* chairs in front of the fireplace—*the* very chair that I have seen all the heavyweight world leaders sit in. President Bush was very friendly, and in the end I found myself sitting on the floor scratching First Dog Millie's belly and discussing flea control with the President of the United States. I recently learned that the reason we waited so long was because the President was in a car on his way to an appointment when he learned that we were there and were waiting for him to get back.

Once, a few years after the Gulf War, while in Qatar for an endurance horse race, we were invited to dine with President Bush and the Crown Prince. Somehow, in the small, organized capital city of Doha, we got lost and couldn't find the seaside palace where the dinner was to be held. We found the city palace, but the security men there didn't as a rule give out directions to strangers, so we found ourselves going around in circles for a good thirty minutes. The palace security didn't find it funny at all when we showed up again for the fourth time. They sent us on our way, in an opposite direction from the palace. Just as we were pulling out of a filling station with yet another set of directions, our car was cut off by a big Mercedes. "That was rude!" I said to Steve, our companion and driver during our stay.

"It's Sheik Abdullah, the Crown Prince," he said with relief. He rolled down his window to try to get the attention of the drivers and bodyguards. A big black window rolled down slowly, and the Crown Prince, recognizing us, smiled and said that we could follow him. "But stay close," he added.

"Stay close" meant flying through Doha on a version of Mr. Toad's Wild Ride. We were the fourth car of a six-vehicle motorcade. Steve nervously did his best to keep up. I was riding shotgun and found the ride thrilling. The drivers were fantastic. My stepfather, Bobby Bass, one of Hollywood's legendary stunt coordinators, who married my mom in 1982, teaches evasive driving. He's told me many times about "situation awareness" and "spotters" and "closing the gap." But I'd never seen any of it outside of his movies, like *Black Rain* and *Lethal Weapon*. The chase car directly in front of us rode outrigger style, veering back and forth, from side to side, a mere three inches off the back bumper of the Crown Prince's car.

Dinner was fascinating and interesting until I put my foot in my mouth and brought up the sore subject of Ross Perot. But the President was gracious and charming and mentioned that he had met my sister, Kelly, at the Kentucky Derby earlier in the year. He asked how her two children were, and I was amazed that he remembered so much about her. "But I was there too," I said. He laughed and apologized for not remembering that I was standing right next to Kelly when we all met.

"Oh, that's all right," I said. "Kelly will love this. The President remembered meeting her and not me. She'll never let me live this one down!"

At first, during the 2000 primaries, I was warned not to make my endorsement for the younger Bush public. "You'll never work in Hollywood again," a well-known actor, who wishes to remain nameless, told me.

"What are you talking about?"

"The business is so liberal," he said. "You'll be blacklisted."

Uh-oh, I thought, *not again*. "That's crazy!" I said.

"It's true. If you don't believe me, ask—" He ran down a list of famous names.

"I can't believe people would be that shallow," I said.

"Can you believe you just said that about *Hollywood?*" asked the actor.

"It's un-American!" I said.

Again and again, I was warned not to go public about my politics, which did nothing but make me more determined than ever to speak my mind.

I was "outed" on Chris Matthews's MSNBC show, *Hardball*. It's my favorite political show and the one that I make a point to stop whatever I'm doing at 5:00 P.M. to watch. "Gotta go catch Chris," I'll say. Chris is *it*. And I'm not the only one with a bit of a crush on him. Women are always coming up to me and asking, "You've met Chris Matthews, right?"

"Yes, I've done the show a couple of times," I'll say.

"Is he as attractive as he looks on TV?" they'll ask.

"Yes, even more so. Did you know he's very tall?"

"Oh . . . That's good to know."

I love the format of the show. Chris is fast, funny, and tough, and at the end of the hour I always feel I've gotten the bottom line on the issues. All good reasons to watch *Hardball*. But what was I thinking when I agreed to be *on* the show? It's called *Hardball* because it is!

Chris can be gentle, I'll vouch for that, because he must have noticed my panicked deer-in-the-headlights expression when the show started. By now, I had been a working actress for twenty years, and I was pretty adept at interviews. Nothing threw me anymore. I'd heard it all. If a journalist tried to shock me with a first question like "Why did you take off your clothes in the film?" I knew exactly what to do. In the old days, I would actually sit and attempt to defend myself or justify that the nude scene was "integral to the film." But I've since reached a comfort level where I could tell him to stick it and show him the door.

Actors get very good at talking about themselves and promoting their latest film. But when it comes to politics, well, that's an entirely different arena. *"What the hell am I doing here?"* was all I could think when Chris asked me why I was a Republican and my views on different issues. I knew what I felt and why, but I hadn't ever really articulated my thoughts before. Talking politics required a new vocabulary, different from the usual Hollywood lexicon of "me," "my latest film," "the genre," "me," "more about me," and "mine." Here I was, stuttering and stammering my way through education, healthcare, and compassionate conservatism on *Hardball*. I must have been out of my mind!

My terror wasn't because I thought I might make a fool of myself. I've done that often enough; falling down the stairs at an awards ceremony doesn't even phase me anymore. But I could be a minor embarrassment to the George W. campaign. The last thing he needed in April 2000 was a dumb blonde, who didn't know what she was talking about, speaking about his policies. We've all seen celebrities do this and wondered, *Why don't they just stick to what they know?*

With Chris holding my hand (figuratively), I squeaked through my first appearance on *Hardball*.

Next, I was asked by the campaign if I would speak at the Republican National Convention in Philadelphia. Naturally, I said that I would be honored.

A couple of weeks later, I was asked if I would introduce my district's assemblyman, Abel Maldonado.

"Yes, that would be wonderful. I know Abel and think so much of him," I said. Then I was told, "He's going to be giving his speech in Spanish; the first time any speech has been given in a foreign language at any convention, Republican or Democrat."

"What a good idea!" I said. After all, I added, I live in an agricultural area of California with a large Spanish-speaking population.

"Would you consider making your introduction first in English and then in Spanish?" I was asked.

"Sure . . ."

Here I go again, I thought. I speak a little Spanish but am not fluent enough to be speaking to the millions of people who would be watching the convention. But as a California girl, I really wanted to be part of this idea of speaking directly to the people I lived with every day.

The convention was, of course, a huge event, and I spent the first two days seeing friends and acquaintances I'd made from the 1996 Bob Dole/Jack Kemp campaign, as well as making new ones. I had a chance to visit with George and Barbara Bush, Jack and Joanne Kemp, General Colin Powell, General Norman Schwarzkopf, John McCain, Dr. Condoleezza Rice, and Dick and Lynne Cheney. Forgive me for dropping names, but the surfer girl in me is still thrown when these heroes recognize me or call me their friend.

The last night of the convention, at 8:00 P.M., prime time, I found myself backstage with a very cool and composed Abel

Maldonado. I was in a daze, wondering what I was going to do out there on stage. I really had no idea whether I could pull it off. How horrible it would be for *the blonde* to screw up the Spanish. Thank God the applause was huge when I came out on that stage and endured the long walk in my four-inch Stuart Weitzman heels (without falling) specially dyed to go with the Richard Tyler suit chosen for the occasion. (These things give girls much confidence.) The California delegation, right in front of my podium, went wild. I was so grateful and buoyed by them that I happily got through my little introduction and only messed up the pronunciation of one vowel in Spanish.

My participation in the campaign gradually gained speed over the next three months. I began putting my new vocabulary to use on more and more political TV and radio talk shows, and in the papers. I started traveling all over the country, speaking at luncheons, dinners, shelters, and get-out-the-vote rallies, always keenly aware that I was just another volunteer expressing my personal enthusiasm for the candidate and his issues. I find the influence celebrities have on our society misplaced.

The last week was spent with the candidate. Well, sort of. I never spent any significant face-to-face time with George W. Bush. It wasn't necessary. Like all the other grassroots volunteers, I believed in him and his solutions to the big problems our country faces. I joined up with Wayne Newton and his beautiful wife, Kathleen, who had offered their time and their plane. We hustled from rally to rally all over the country, and soon Wayne and I had our little act down pretty good. Wayne can entertain, sing, and tell jokes. Me? I learned to give a halfway decent pep talk. Then, if George W. was running late, Wayne would sing another song, and I could always go out and autograph Bush 2000 banners.

Wayne's turboprop was slightly slower than the campaign's big jet. So that meant that when George W. and Laura arrived, we would all greet each other onstage, and the Governor and Mrs. Bush would thank us for our efforts. Wayne and Kat and I would run offstage and take a police escort to the airport, where Wayne's plane would be revved up and ready for takeoff. It was the only way for us to get to the next event, to warm up the crowd before George W. arrived. If the next venue was too far away, we would leapfrog to the stop after that.

Some of the rallies were thrilling: thousands of screaming people, so believing that the country was going to be better because of George W. On Election Day, we went to five cities in five states, ending up in Austin, Texas, with the polls saying the race was too close to call.

We stayed up all night in the rainy cold, watching the drama of the election bouncing back and forth. At one point, we all lined up in front of the stage because the Secret Service said that "he" was coming out in twenty minutes. *Wow*, I thought, *this is really happening. Here I am, and the new president of the United States of America will be right there in front of me. This is history!*

Then, of course, we waited and waited, and my opportunity to witness history was put on hold for five weeks. I went straight to the Austin airport to fly back to L.A. and then to the studio, where I was doing a guest appearance on a sitcom.

So, I'd proved my friend wrong; thus far, anyway. I was working, despite having let myself become known as a Republican. But—and this is a big *but*—many members of the cast and crew came up to me and whispered that I was courageous to stand up for what I believe. They also whispered, *"I voted for Bush. But don't tell anyone. I'll lose my job."*

If there is no discrimination against Republicans in Hollywood, the *impression* that discrimination exists is so strong that the result is the same. Many people hide their beliefs and for whom they voted. I think it's disgraceful and something that, if I were a Democrat, I would want to correct.

Finally, with the election drama over, I was invited to the inauguration, where Wayne and I were reunited onstage to emcee the candlelight dinner. On Inauguration Day, I appeared on *Hardball* again. This time it was a little easier, but it was still *Hardball*. Then I went to ride in the inaugural parade. As I was walking to my "celebrity vehicle," I passed an entry of retired Vietnam helicopter pilots. They had about five C-Company helicopters that were being pulled by jeeps in the parade. I stopped to talk to them, and they told me stories of service and showed me some bullet holes in the chopper that I was standing beside. "I want to ride with you guys!" I said.

"Sure!" they chorused. The men proceeded to rerig the pilot's door so that I could sit on the armrest and hang out to wave to the crowd.

Just then, some Secret Service agents came hustling up. "I'm sorry, Ms. Derek," said one, "but you have to ride in your assigned vehicle. You're not cleared to be here."

"No, I think I'd rather stay here," I said. "Can't you talk to someone?"

I had gotten a little spoiled during the campaign, with all-access clearance and motorcades and all.

"I'm sorry, ma'am," he said, urging me to return to my assigned vehicle.

"You're not taking her anywhere!" the pilots protested, holding me by the shoulders.

An agent spoke into his wrist, then turned to me, and said, "Have a nice parade, ma'am."

It was wonderful riding with the pilots, and they seemed happy to have me with them. The bystanders saluted and called out "Thank you!" to the pilots as we passed.

"Thank you for letting me ride with you," I told the pilots. "I'm so happy to see this."

"This is the best treatment we've ever had, Bo," they said.

"What do you mean?"

"Some people don't know how to treat us," one of them explained. "I've seen them saluting and applauding vets from other wars, but when they see us they stop and stare or look down. And then some people even boo us."

"I'm so sorry . . ." I said.

As we approached the viewing stand, the pilots, standing on the skids, stiffened and saluted the President. The President responded in kind, with great respect to the pilots. I was starting to cry at the significance of it all, when I saw the president point my way and say to his father, "Look, there's Bo!" Everyone on the viewing stand waved to me, and I was overcome by it all when one of the pilots put his arm around me and said, "Isn't this great!?"

Yes, it was. The whole experience of getting involved in the campaign was great. I love this country more, I'm sure, because I've traveled and worked so much overseas. Having seen just about all the *-isms* in the world firsthand, I've come to my own conclusions about what works and what doesn't.

I made so many friendships during the campaign, friendships that I hope last my lifetime. Being declared "intelligent" was a lovely bonus. Maybe I should have made an attempt to change my image sooner, because this is nice.

TWENTY

I can hear Centauro screaming in the barn. He's upset, and I go
down and check on him. I love strolling down to the barn late at
night. I turn on the light and see the bats darting around catching
insects. All the horses look out, their eyes squinting from the sudden
bright light.

Centauro is pacing back and forth and tossing his head. He lets
out a thunderous cry. There is a mare in heat about a quarter of a
mile away, and he smelled her today when the wind was just right.
There was no mistaking her scent. He's been calling to her all
night.

When I enter the stall, I can see that he is hot. His chest is lathered with white foam. His nostrils are flared. I stand in his way until
he stops pacing and comes to me. I begin to stroke his face and try to
soothe him with my voice. "*Shhhh, quieto,*" I say. I run my hands
along the firm crest of his neck. It's arched and wet, and I kiss it. It's
salty and nice. His veins are engorged with blood. I continue to run
my hands down his forelegs. His cannon bones are long because he is

Spanish. His pasterns are hot, and I can feel his pulse there, which is bad. But they are not swollen, which is good.

Centauro is utterly beautiful, named for the way his long neck comes straight up out of his shoulders, like the half-man, half-horse centaur of ancient mythology. My girlfriend CiCi says, "He's not a horse! He's a creature!" His coat is a dark bay color, flecked with white around his flanks and tail. A seventeenth-century author wrote: "All bays are good, the best of all being dark bays and those that are white-ticked or have white hairs at the root of the tail, for they are courageous and noble." That describes Centauro well.

My hands go back up his legs and move on to his body. His barrel is deep and strong because he was bred for centuries to be a saddle horse. Tomorrow he will carry me with such strength and grace. I wipe the foam from his chest. "Easy, *guapo*," I say, working my way along his top line to his loins. I stroke his back, which can easily carry a large man. (My 110 pounds is nothing for him.) I lean up against him and use my whole arm and chest to feel the beautiful slope of his hindquarters, the croup, and haunches. They are round and powerful, and they propel us effortlessly up steep hills.

He has quieted somewhat, so I go back to his face. He puts his nostrils to my mouth and sucks in my breath. His muzzle is so soft, like velvet, and he begins to nuzzle me all over my face. He works his way around to my ears and the back of my neck. I cup my hands over each eye, and it seems to calm him. His beautiful deep brown liquid eyes look to me for comfort. My fingers find his *stud bumps*, a protrusion of bone over his eyes. All horses have this bone, but it is exaggerated in a stallion. There is a depression just above the stud bumps, and I kiss him there—funny that my lips fit perfectly in that hollow.

He finally drops his head, and I stroke his ears from the base to the tips. Centauro has little horns that grow from the base of his ears; proof that he is pure *Cartujano*. His precious bloodlines can be traced back to the seventeenth century and to the monks of *La Cartuja de Jerez*, who were dedicated to breeding these Spanish horses.

Centauro's breathing has slowed, and he lays the length of his forehead against my chest. His hot breath goes right through my shirt, and I can feel it on my belly.

I fell in love this year.

It was a flat-on-your-face, obsessive, unhealthy, crazy love. Why did love have to come along and ruin everything? I was doing so well. I was so proud of the new me: the independent, self-sufficient, making-my-own-way me. I made my own decisions—right, wrong, big, small—all by myself.

I was adjusting very well to being a middle-aged woman. I was no longer shocked by the new wrinkles that have appeared every friggin' day since I'd turned forty-two (that was my bad year). I was dealing with my herniated disc and all the new aches and pains that come to you in your forties if you've lived an active life.

I was enjoying all the free time I had. I could read a big, fat book all the way through if I wanted. Get up whenever I wanted. Husbands take so much time. But then . . .

It was those damn orange blossoms again.

I was slightly curious that I hadn't been attracted to a man for the years since John's death, but only slightly. I chalked it up to having already met my soul mate. Some never do, and it would be greedy of me to think that I could find another. I was in the process of shamelessly fashioning my new single life after Ursula's. A girl would be lucky to have a life half as adventurous and exciting as hers: traveling the world, collecting an interesting group of friends, and, as Urs says, "having my freedom." Freedom, she believes, means never having to rely on a man for anything.

I was thinking that I might even live in Europe for a while. I could learn a new language and absorb some culture. Like so many Americans, I don't speak a second language, which is an embarrassment to me, as I spend so much time overseas. I'm always going on and on like a broken record about how much I love Spain. There is nothing keeping me in the United States anymore.

I'd become my friends' favorite *project*. "Don't worry about me," I'd say. "I'm fine, I'm happy, I'm not lonely at all. I'm too *busy* to be lonely."

To which they'd all reply, "Bo, how are you ever going to meet someone with that attitude? You'll end up alone!"

"Please stop trying to set me up," I'd tell them. "I'd rather spend my free time with good friends or at home in bed with my dogs and a good book than to spend an evening with a stranger, feeling awkward and tortured trying to make conversation." It was the God's truth.

If they persisted, I'd add, "Look, maybe someday I'll be shot by Cupid's arrow. But until then, leave me alone."

The orange blossoms were in bloom in Seville in November 2000, when I arrived with Shehkar and Ursula for the Spanish Horse International Salon. Featuring fifteen hundred Andalusian horses, it is the largest single-breed horse show in the world. This was Ursula's first visit to the south of Spain, and I enjoyed showing her the city and introducing her to my Spanish friends. Urs has been very kind to share her life and her friends with me, and we travel together often.

We all spent a particularly beautiful Hemingway-esque day together looking at horses and brave bulls, drinking sherry, eating olives, and laughing with some of Papa's old friends. At sunset we ended up at the home of a matador friend whose ranch and bodega is especially gorgeous. It's a converted seventeenth-century convent with a courtyard, which, like every courtyard in Andalusia, is filled with orange trees.

As we were admiring the beauty of the spot and the night, the scent from the blossoms came wafting across the cobblestones. This time the scent triggered a sudden, terrible loneliness within me. It wasn't from missing John, although we had been together in this same courtyard years before. It was my very own aloneness.

I was walking with a very attractive bullfighter, and I suddenly felt his closeness as he reached up to pull an orange off the tree for me. He was very young—so young that I'd just seen a picture in the house of the two of us together when I was well into adulthood and he was seven—which quickly snuffed out any romantic thoughts I might have entertained. We shared the orange, which, of course, was perfectly delicious, and, like a scene from a hokey romantic novel, its juice ran down my chin. The experience left me feeling so sad and small and lonely and solitary. Once again, I was being readied for a change.

I wasn't back home three days when I fell in love at first sight. No Cupid's arrow for me. No, I was hit over the head with a sledgehammer. Me! The Ice Queen. It was the beginning of the most miserable time of my life.

From the moment I met him, I found myself in a sorry state. I was forty-four years old but equipped with the emotional experience of a seventeen-year-old, my age when I fell in love with John. I had never learned to put all my feelings in perspective. Never learned to protect myself. I was a bundle of raw emotions, all sparking and lighting.

And just my luck, I fell for a guy who was much too busy for me: a lawyer with an ex-wife, a daughter, and important change-the-world projects. It wasn't his fault that I fell so hard. No, I did this all on my own.

"But isn't it wonderful to have all those emotions again, Bo?" my friends, so excited for me, would ask.

"No," I'd say. "I hate this! All these stupid feelings."

"But you're alive!" they'd counter.

"I was so much happier when I was all nice and numb."

Lovesick, lovelorn, disheartened, heartbroken—all the silly clichés suddenly described exactly how I felt. I could always have a good cry at a sentimental movie, but this was ridiculous! Hearing someone sing left me a blubbering idiot. I wonder how many other people have cried at a Huey Lewis concert?

I bored my girlfriends to no end with my laments. For months, my heart jumped when the phone rang. It was never him. I kept thinking, *If only I could put this much attention and concentration (all right, obsession) into my work, I'd probably be very successful.*

"Stop sighing!" Kerry scolded as I moped around the house.

"Why doesn't he call?" I'd ask her for the umpteenth time.

"Because he's busy, and you're not his priority," Kerry would say. "You're just . . . Back-burner Bo!" And she'd laugh.

Overall, screw feeling alive! The whole experience has left me restless and unhappy, and I can't think of anything good that came of it. I've *got* to get over what's-his-name. I have enough on my plate, worrying about what will become of me. What's wrong with me? What will I do? Why even get out of bed in the morning? How will I survive? Will I make the transition from movie star to working actor? Not many people do. Do I have the talent for it? I really don't know. Talent was never required before. What's an aging sex symbol to do?

I had a long talk with Gerry Spence one night. Gerry Spence: the famous trial attorney who has never lost a criminal case; who wears buckskin coats handmade by his wife, Imaging; the author of more than a dozen books so I *know* he writes from deep down in his soul. Gerry can see right through me—see what I am hiding—and can bring me to tears and a long-overdue cry. Gerry can set me straight when I begin to flounder. This particular night I was in a pretty-good-sized funk—flopping around, gills gasping—about my life and future.

I absolutely adore this man in a way that confuses me, and beautiful Imaging doesn't even seem to mind.

Although I had come to dinner for my fix—to let Gerry poke around all my soft spots—I was dodging and sidestepping and laughing and being silly most of the night. Then Gerry mused aloud how he'd been thinking that he wasn't responsible for his many accomplishments.

"Gerry that's not true," I argued. "Look what you have done for so many people."

"No," he said, "I can't take credit for any of that. My parents gave me my good health and my intelligence, which is what has allowed me to become successful."

"But, Gerry, look what you've *done* with what you have," I said, trying to keep my voice low. It gets shrill, which is a problem I have. "You must be proud of that. You know you could be the best scum-sucking attorney, but instead you help the little people!"

He wouldn't hear it. "My decisions are a product of what my parents taught me and the result of all my life experiences," he said. "I really had no choice, and I've had nothing to do with all those good things that have come to me."

The conversation continued until I could argue no further. And I *love* to argue with Gerry! Then he zeroed in on my sagging spirits and opened some hidden wounds. I had a nice little weep and felt like an idiot for feeling sorry for myself. Since then, I've been thinking about what he was trying to get me to understand and apply to my life: that all of us are products of our genetics and life experience. I've concluded that if this is true for Gerry, I just might be the poster child for his theory.

I judge myself by those I call friends. Those I love and care about. Those I admire and in some cases almost worship. They validate me. They affirm that I somewhat resemble the kind of person that I would like to be. And it's still awfully good to be Bo. Still better than being king! I have most of the same perks as royalty anyway. If I should become interested in something, all doors open for me, all because I was on a movie screen for a few minutes. I've met so many of my heroes: world leaders, movers and shakers, great writers and artists. General Norman Schwarzkopf taught me to play blackjack. I can literally be Queen for a Day. And whenever I get tired of all the fun and excitement, I can disappear. Go home. Turn it all off. Come back to Ramon Becerra's arena, where it's more important how I ride than who I am.

And today, when it comes to riding, I'm still a big fat nobody, trotting Gaiata around and around in endless circles, trying to persuade my horse to relax enough to pull off the perfect pirouette. "Ramon, I've been doing pirouettes for years!" I shout. "What's up now?"

"You're all messed up," he says. "You're tense and tight. She can feel it in your seat. What's bothering you?"

"Only a thousand stupid things."

Ramon laughs at me. "Let everything go," he says. "Take off her saddle and take her out into the hills for the rest of the day. Just the two of you. Don't worry. You'll get your seat back."

Indeed. Somehow, some way, I always do.

PHOTOGRAPH CAPTIONS

PHOTOGRAPH CREDITS